AFRICAN
TEMPLES
OF THE
ANUNNAKI

■ ■ ■

Scholars have told us that the first civilization
on Earth emerged in a land called Sumer
some 6,000 years ago. Recent archaeological findings
suggest that the Sumerians inherited some of their
knowledge from a far earlier civilization
that emerged many thousands of years before them in
southern Africa—the Cradle of Humankind.

AFRICAN TEMPLES
OF THE
ANUNNAKI

The Lost Technologies of the Gold Mines of Enki

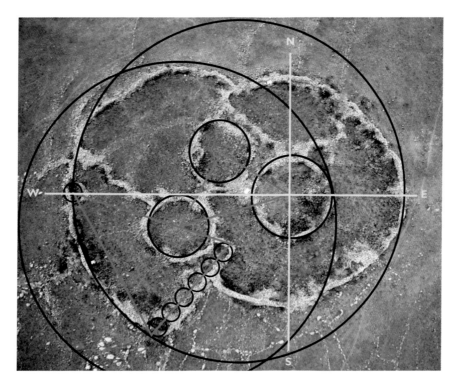

MICHAEL TELLINGER

Photographs by Johan Heine and Michael Tellinger

Bear & Company
Rochester, Vermont • Toronto, Canada

Bear & Company
One Park Street
Rochester, Vermont 05767
www.BearandCompanyBooks.com

Bear & Company is a division of Inner Traditions International

Library of Congress Cataloging-in-Publication Data
Tellinger, Michael.
  African temples of the Anunnaki : the lost technologies of the gold mines of Enki /
Michael Tellinger.
       p. cm.
  "Originally published in South Africa in 2009 by Zulu Planet Publishers under the title
Temples of the African Gods: Revealing the Ancient Hidden Ruins of Southern Africa."
  Summary: "Archaeological proof of the advanced civilization on the southern tip of Africa
that preceded Sumer and Egypt by 200,000 years"—Provided by publisher.
  Includes bibliographical references.
  ISBN 978-1-59143-150-3 (pbk.)
  1. Archaeology and religion—South Africa. 2. Cradle of Humankind World Heritage Site
(South Africa) 3. South Africa—Antiquities. 4. South Africa—History. I. Title.
  BL65.A72T44 2013
  968.00901—dc23

                                                                        2012039273

Printed and bound in India by Replika Press, Pvt. Ltd.

10   9   8   7   6

Text design and layout by Virginia Scott Bowman
This book was typeset in Garamond Premier Pro and Gill Sans with Centaur used as the
display typeface

To send correspondence to the author of this book, mail a first-class letter to the author c/o
Inner Traditions • Bear & Company, One Park Street, Rochester, VT 05767, and we will
forward the communication, or contact the author directly at **www.michaeltellinger.com**.

Contents

Foreword by Professor Pieter Wagener ▪ vii

Preface ▪ ix

Introduction: Ancient Human History ▪ 1

Visionaries ▪ 3

Hidden History ▪ 16

Human Origins and Mythology ▪ 22

Cornerstones of Our Beliefs ▪ 25

The Walls ▪ 28

Obsession with the Stars ▪ 52

Adam's Calendar ▪ 60

South African Sphinx ▪ 65

Adam's Pyramids ▪ 69

Measurements ▪ 73

The Flood ▪ 79

Lost Cities—Vanished Civilizations ▪ 81

Calculating the Impossible ▪ 90

The Oldest Agricultural Terraces ▪ 96

Ancient Roads and Mysterious Energy ▪ 102

Ancient Levitation Device and White Powder of Gold ▪ 112

Shapes of Ruins as Energy Devices ▪ 116

Population Mystery ▪ 124

From Stone Age to Iron Age ▪ 127

Quest for Gold ▪ 143

Sumerian Tablets ▪ 154

The African-Sumerian Connection ▪ 160

Petroglyphs ▪ 165

Aerial Views ▪ 174

Monoliths ▪ 201

Giants, Tools, and Other Anomalies ▪ 216

Conclusion ▪ 223

Resources ▪ 225

Bibliography ▪ 226

Foreword

AUTHOR MICHAEL TELLINGER and pilot and photographer Johan Heine are two of the bravest persons I know. Bravery can be associated with foolishness, but the bravery of this scientist and pilot stems from a conviction based on meticulous research. At the start of this millennium, their findings will inaugurate a dramatic new understanding of the history of mankind over the past 100 millennia. This understanding will affect the foundations of human understanding in all its facets, but especially in philosophy, psychology, history, and religion. Accordingly, their bravery will be put to severe test. Innovators are rarely appreciated, and gratitude takes a long time in coming. One may wonder,

■ *Close-up of one of the mysterious and intriguing stone structures examined by the author*

therefore, why they go to all the trouble. But that is the stuff that makes a true scientist.

When the reader looks at the photographs in this book his first reaction is to ask why no one before has taken a serious look at these thousands of structures and petroglyphs. The answer is that we become complacent when other people tell us that there is nothing significant about them. This book is about to demolish that complacency and make every reader—believer or not—uncomfortable about the origins of our civilization. Even worse, the reader could deduce that some of our ancestors were much smarter than we are today.

Ex Africa semper aliquid novi.
Out of Africa always something new.

PIETER WAGENER, PH.D., L.L.D.

Pieter Wagener holds bachelor's degrees in philosophy, languages, and music; master's degrees in chemistry, mathematics, physics, and law; and doctorates in applied mathematics and law. His main research interests are anthropaleontology and gravitational theory, and his research articles have been published in a number of scientific and humanity journals. Presently he is writing a history of physics in South Africa and a book, *In Search of Gods and Angels,* which traces the origin of the ancient advanced societies to southern Africa.

Preface

MY LIFE CHANGED irreversibly around April 2007 when I met Johan Heine in Pretoria. He came to see my presentation on *Slave Species of the Gods,* not realizing that I was a South African author. After the presentation he asked if I would like to see some strange stone structures and ruins in South Africa, at which point he whipped out his laptop and started showing me his collection of aerial photographs that he had been taking for at least fifteen years.

Just like everyone does when they first encounter these mysterious circular stone structures, I was riveted. I could not fathom that this had never been exposed by our historians and archaeologists. It was at that moment that I was overcome by a strong sense that these structures are inextricably linked to everything I had been writing about in *Slave Species of the Gods.* Six months later Johan and I got together again, this time for me to see these ruins in real life—from one of the helicopters used by his forestry fire fighting company.

Even from our first outing together it became clear that we would get very little interest or support from the mainstream academia in South Africa. The day that we took off to fly over the ruins, Johan had invited a whole host of historians, archaeologists, and geologists from the various universities in South Africa. Not one of them took up his generous offer of being flown over the ruins—an experience that millions would cherish. I was the only one to arrive.

With the original help from Dr. Cyril Hromnik—whose contribution to the untold history of southern Africa is captured in his wonderful 1981 book, *Indo-Africa*—Johan measured and analyzed several of the ruins. This was the first real breakthrough in recognizing that these stone ruins are not just ordinary structures but are carefully aligned to the movement of the sun, solstices, and equinoxes—clearly a premeditated feature, and a sign of intelligence.

All my gratitude goes out to Johan and his wife, Lizette, for their many years of commitment while photographing the ruins and trying to bring their

significance to the attention of the South African academia, and also for shar-
ing all his initial knowledge with me.

I also acknowledge the MaKomati Foundation and Dr. Cyril Hromnik,
whose brilliant insight into the activity and influence of the MaKomati people in southern Africa over the past several thousand years has changed our
view of history. This astute academic researcher was pretty much excommu-
nicated by the academic fraternity in South Africa because of his alternative

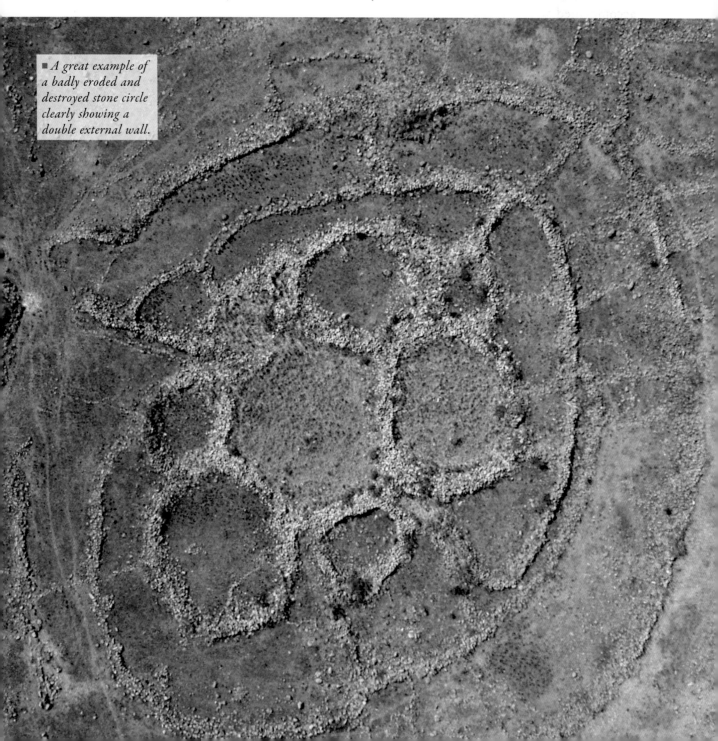

■ *A great example of a badly eroded and destroyed stone circle clearly showing a double external wall.*

views. His work should be taught and not hidden from the young students hungry for truth.

My ongoing research, findings, and conclusions would not have been possible without the immense influence of Johan Heine, Cyril Hromnik, and the MaKomati Foundation—who empowered me with their support and material to do the work that I have done.

In any process of research and discovery there is a great deal of work accompanied with the ups and downs that swing between depression and ecstasy. A journey like this is not an easy one and could not be accomplished without the continuous support from a multitude of individuals and organizations, in addition to those I have already named. Some people contributed to these discoveries in many ways, completely unaware of their actions. I compiled a list of those people who crossed my path in the process of making these startling discoveries. To all of you, and those whom I may have omitted, I extend my most sincere gratitude. Please keep exploring, and spread your own passion.

Sincere thanks go to Paul van Niekerk and all the farmers whose land was used in this exploration, Brian Young, Bruce and Roelie Pretorius, Dr. Gideon Groenewald, Mike van Niekerk, Theunis and Ben Niewoudt, Linda Pampallis, Angie Shackleford, Matt Louw, Thompsons Travel, Win Saunders, Nicola Wilson, Rudi and Petro du Plessis, Reinette van Niekerk, the people of Kaapschehoop, Andy Stadler, Johan Zietsman, Sappi Ltd. and Richard McArthy, Richard Green, Richard Wade, Willemien Hodgkinson, Fred Favar and the Working on Fire team, Gustav and Alex van Rensburg, DJ van Tonder, Willem de Swart, John Wallington, Frans Kruger, George van Gils, Merwyn Williams, Darryl Freeman, Peter and Rose Hobson, Nick van Noordwyk, Lily Hattingh, Peter Batistich, Bill Maliepaard, Junita Coetzee, Ted Loukes, Louise Clarke, the people of Waterval Boven, and many more.

Ancient Human History

THE ANCIENT HISTORY of southern Africa is one of the great mysteries of humankind. While the world has become obsessed with places like Egypt, Mesopotamia, Mexico, and other popularized locations, very few have paid the same kind of attention to the real Cradle of Humankind—southern Africa. The discoveries we have been making in southern Africa since 2003 are so astonishing that they will require a dramatic paradigm shift in our perception of human history. History is written by the victors,

■ *Ancient structure stretching across the landscape, its stones and mysteries still intact*

and it is evident that it has been dramatically skewed by its authors over many centuries. Therefore, we should assume that we actually know very little about the real path that brought us to this point in our human history. We need to set aside preconceived ideas and any rosy pictures we harbor about who we are and where we come from, because the research is delivering answers that some of us may not be ready to accept. It is imperative that we follow the clues and not hide any evidence simply because it does not fit the picture of human history as it was painted for us by historians—who may not have had all the pieces of the puzzle.

This book is a continuation of my research into our murky origins as a species—a species that is rapidly losing its way and destroying its own planet. This book has been compiled simply to spark the interest of those who are ready to accept a new alternative to the conventional; it presents new possibilities that may have seemed unthinkable until now. I am certain that there are not too many people on Earth today who are deeply happy with the way the world has turned out. A new understanding of the real history of humankind may just provide some of the answers we have been searching for and deliver a new sense of comfort for many who feel betrayed by our historians—and especially by our religions.

Visionaries

MAINSTREAM HISTORY TELLS a simple, familiar story: the first civilization on Earth was in Sumer, between the Tigris and Euphrates Rivers, some 6,000 years ago. This book presents and offers insights into some of the recent archaeological discoveries in southern Africa, which suggest that the Sumerians and even the Egyptians inherited much of their knowledge from an earlier civilization that emerged in our ancient past.

Sanusi Credo Mutwa is probably South Africa's most treasured visionary—he is a shaman and *sangoma*.* For many years Credo has been talking about

■ *Sanusi Credo Mutwa—an unsung hero who has been a guiding light of wisdom for millions of people on this confused planet*

**Sangoma is a term for a traditional healer of southern Africa. In the past it specifically referred to one who practiced arts of divination for healing, as opposed to an *inyanga,* who healed through medicinal plants. However, nowadays the terms have become more fluid, and most traditional healers practice a mix of these arts.*

■ *Credo's reminder of Africa's great hidden legacy*

the ancient civilizations that existed here in South Africa; his assertions caused many so-called educated scholars to scoff. When Johan Heine discovered the ancient stone calendar (Adam's Calendar) at Kaapsche Hoop in South Africa in 2003, as you will see in the "Adam's Calendar" chapter, he could never have imagined that this would be the spark that started the sudden emergence of archaeological proof to vindicate the statements of Baba Credo Mutwa.

Proof comes in the form of large stone monolith statues, petroglyphs, and symbols discovered in Mpumalanga and other parts of South Africa, which were previously believed to be of Sumerian and Egyptian origins. My conclusions are not only based on the many convincing artifacts I have accumulated and the staggering ages ascribed to them but also on the transcripts of the Sumerian tablets themselves. These tablets are the oldest written record of human history; the constant reference to southern Africa leaves little doubt that there was a lot of activity in this region long before Sumer or Egypt were established. The tablets make it very clear that the first civilization emerged many thousands of years ago in a land they called the ABZU—the land of the FIRST people in southern Africa—where the gold came from.

When I first started researching the stone ruins in South Africa in late 2007, I never imagined that I had stumbled upon what might be the most explosive missing piece of the puzzle of our human origins. But as the months and years went by, it slowly became very clear that the many strange

tools and artifacts I had been collecting would become the physical evidence and the vital clues that would enable us to complete the story.

It seems that many great discoveries are made inadvertently by travelers and explorers who keep their eyes open and are able to recognize unusual objects or anomalies in their surroundings. This was certainly the case with Johan Heine when he saw the strange arrangement of stones from the airplane he was flying. What he encountered turned out to be a complex ancient calendar with many hidden secrets yet to be discovered.

When I first came face to face with the stone ruins and the stone calendar, which I later called Adam's Calendar, I had an overwhelming sense that these ruins were somehow connected to the information that I presented in *Slave Species of the Gods.* I relocated my life from Johannesburg to the small town of Waterval Boven in the province of Mpumalanga to be able to focus on my new obsession—the vanished civilizations of South Africa.

This small, impoverished railway town is located right in the heart of the most dense part of the stone ruins; it is about forty minutes away from Adam's Calendar, which is located farther east at the small mountaintop village of Kaapsche Hoop. The settlements of Waterval Boven and Waterval Onder (meaning "waterfall above" and "waterfall below") became famous during the South African War (Anglo-Boer War, 1899–1902). This war was fought between the British Empire and about 80,000 Boere (farmers) and

■ *Waterval Boven in the distance and several ruins in the foreground with mysterious small circles inside the walls and structure of a larger stone circle*

many thousands of black South Africans, who represented two independent Boer republics: the South African Republic (Transvaal Republic) and the Orange Free State. Many of these fighters pledged allegiance to Paul Kruger, the president of the Transvaal Republic. The little house where Kruger stayed for a few months and inspired the Boer commandos is now a humble museum located at Waterval Onder. Kruger is remembered for two reasons: the Kruger Park and Krugerrands. His name will forever be synonymous with gold—and this should be no surprise to anyone.

The reason why I bring up this part of South African history is because, to date, this remains the most expensive war that the British Empire has ever

■ *The Krugerrand, a South African gold coin depicting Paul Kruger*

fought. They threw everything they could at this problem in the south. An estimated 470,000 British troops were sent to South Africa to deal with the Boer problem. Among them were also Australians, New Zealanders, and Canadians. Their instructions were simple—take control of this part of the world, no matter what the cost. This was a time before the Wright brothers; airplanes did not yet fill the sky. Just compare this number of troops more than 100 years ago, when transport was by ship only, to the number of troops used by the United States and Britain in the Gulf War. In October 2012 there are an estimated 250,000 U.S. troops and 45,000 British troops in the Gulf. This means that there were more British troops in the South African War than there are collectively in the continuing Gulf War in 2012.

This was a quite spectacular achievement on its own: to get that many troops, horses, canons, wagons, weapons, and more to the southern tip of Africa to fight against a band of farmers on horseback. The empire could not lose control of the Orange Free State and Transvaal under any condition. Why? Because of the GOLD!

The little village of Kaapsche Hoop is no exception. It not only plays a key role in the South Africa gold rush that started around 1868, but it also—since

■ *The remains of Kruger's "tea house" on a farm nearby the current museum that was his house. Here, in this clandestine drinking hole, the Boere men would meet to indulge in alcoholic beverages— and probably discuss strategy and plan their next moves.*

Adam's Calendar was rediscovered there in 2003—provides a direct link to our human origins. The story goes that in 1881 a digger by the name of Bernard Chomse was the first to find gold in a streambed near Kaapsche Hoop, which was then named Duiwel's Kantoor ("Devil's Office"). The name came from the outcrop of strangely formed rocks said to look like monsters waiting for the devil. This name, however, did not last very long; by the late 1800s, Kaapsche Hoop became a real frontier gold-mining town bustling with around 15,000 people, with bars and saloons as popularized by countless movies. The largest gold nugget ever found in South Africa was found here in 1912, weighing 175 ounces, or just over 5 kilograms.

This recent quest for gold is simply a continuation of what has been going on here for thousands of years. These past events are directly linked to the more ancient times in southern Africa, of which many people are not aware. Going back thousands of years, this includes the golden kingdom of Monomotapa; the vanished port of Sofala on the coast of Mozambique; the MaKomati people, who were gold merchants and miners from southern India; the Arabic traders that go back to the eighth century AD; the ongoing slave trade that has caused so much misery among humanity for thousands of years; the Queen of Sheba; King Solomon's Mines; and many more mysteries that feed our imagination.

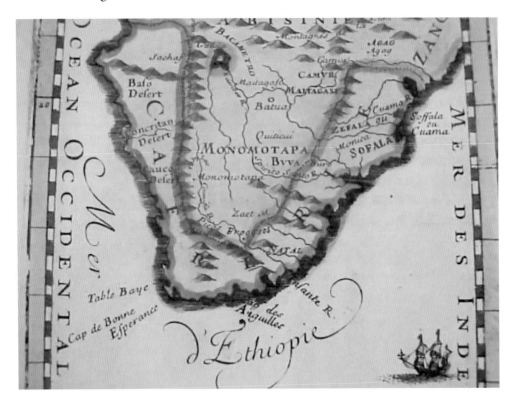

■ *Map showing the golden kingdom of Monomotapa and the vanished port of Sofala*

My research into ancient human history, which includes a new set of circumstances revolving around the origins of humankind, leads me to the conclusion that the British royalty knew all about this gold long before it was rediscovered by modern prospectors in the mid-1800s. I suspect that those in control of the British Empire were simply waiting for the right opportunity to take control of the situation: not allowing the gold to fall under the rule of rogue farmers and settlers with no allegiance to the British crown, which had been passed down the royal bloodline for thousands of years.

To achieve this victory over the Boer army, the British had to go to drastic measures. They adopted the "scorched earth" policy: burning down farms, killing or confiscating livestock, and putting black South Africans and thousands of women and children from the farms into concentration camps scattered across South Africa. It is estimated that at least 34,000 people died in these camps, but the number is most likely much higher. This was the model that was later adapted by Adolf Hitler in his own version of concentration camps.

While millions of people hold on to a deep hatred for Hitler because of what he did to human beings in his concentration camps, it is amazing how few people are aware of the brutality committed in South Africa by the British army—who committed such acts simply because they wanted to take control of the rich gold fields. This is where it always leads when we explore the origins of humankind, because gold is the common denominator in all of human history. No matter how hard we try, we cannot separate our human obsession for gold from the origins of our species. Nowhere is it more evident than in the insane expense and trouble that the British Empire went to in South Africa.

There is one particular battle that took place during the South African War that could have changed the entire history of our modern world. This was the

■ *One of the many concentration camps in South Africa set up by British forces during the South African War (1899–1902)*

battle of Spionkop, near the town of Ladysmith. Spionkop is known as one of the bloodiest battles of the South African War and is often cited as the battle where more men died in one acre of battlefield than in any other war. The incredible thing is that there were three prominent world leaders involved in this battle, representing the Western world, Asia, and Africa. All three had a fundamental effect on global politics and economics that started no less than eight years after this war. They were Mahatma Ghandi, Winston Churchill, and General Louis Botha, probably the most influential commander of the Boer army. If any one of these leaders had been killed, our world would not look the way it does now. The first two names are well known to virtually everyone alive today, but General Botha has somehow escaped even the South African historians' praises for what he really achieved.

On May 16, 1902, in a carefully reasoned speech, Botha persuaded the leaders of the Orange Free State and Transvaal that a decision for peace should be declared while they were still a nation. "Do not let us regard a period of universal burial as the bitter end. If we do, we shall be to blame for national suicide," he said.

In 1910, eight years after losing the war to the British, he was elected as the Union of South Africa's first prime minister. Although many may disagree with my sentiments here, I see a strong similarity between what Botha did in 1910 and what Nelson Mandela did after his release from prison in 1990. They both

■ *Mahatma Ghandi*

■ *General Louis Botha*

■ *Winston Churchill*

swallowed their egos and pride and chose not to continue fighting against the oppressors. By the time Mandela was released he must have known that he was going to be the next president and must have had a personal strategy for what he would do next. Botha could have chosen to go underground and continue a guerrilla war against the British. This kind of activity would have changed the South African landscape dramatically and would have made it very difficult for the empire to control their gold-mining operations. It is difficult to know what backroom deals were struck between Botha and the British, but he chose a peaceful way ahead for South Africa and was elected prime minister to look after the "colony" for King George V of Britain.

The union came to an end when the 1961 constitution was enacted. On May 31, 1961, the country became a republic under the name of the Republic of South Africa. And so the control continues—a different time, a different name, a different leader, slowly rolling from one form of control to the next.

What I find greatly confusing and quite disturbing is a letter written by the early leaders of the African National Congress (ANC) to King George V on December 16, 1918, pledging their allegiance and loyalty. This is an extract of only the first part of a lengthy letter.

Petition to King George V,
from the South African Native National Congress

16 December 1918

Memorial

To His Most Gracious Majesty King George V of Great Britain and Ireland including the Dominions and Colonies, and Emperor of India.

May It Please Your Majesty—

1. We, the Chiefs and delegates assembled at Johannesburg, this 16th day of December, 1918, in the Special Session of the South African Native National Congress, a political body representing the various tribes of the Bantu people in South Africa, record the expression of our satisfaction and thankfulness in the triumph of righteousness in this great war by the victory of the forces of Great Britain, her noble Allies, and the United States of America.

2. We beg to convey to Your Majesty our affectionate loyalty and devotion to Your Majesty's person and Throne and the sincerity of our desire that Divine Blessing and prosperity may attend Your Majesty and all Your Majesty's Dominions in the dawn of a better age.

3. We further express the hope and wish that during Your Majesty's Reign all races and Nations will be treated fairly and with justice, and that there will be no discrimination on account of colour or creed; and will enjoy the right of citizenship, freedom and liberty under your flag.

This kind of declaration of allegiance flies in the face of the principles of a liberation movement, which should represent the absolute liberation of the people from all forms of oppression and control. Africa remains the Cradle of Humankind, and we keep rediscovering critical clues that support this. These clues come in the form of ruins, tools, artifacts, and also genetic research. When we follow the clues as far back as we can, we realize that there was a time when all this control over humanity began: a specific time in human history that remains shrouded in mystery. It was a time when the royal-political bloodlines suddenly appeared on Earth and took control of the rest of humanity.

These bloodlines were equally strong in southern Africa in ancient times, with powerful ancient kingdoms that ruled for hundreds—if not thousands—of years. They mined gold and copper and iron, but somehow they were superseded by their royal cousins in Europe who arrived here in the late 1400s and took control. It is quite shocking when we discover the extent of human manipulation and how far back it actually goes.

What most of us do not realize is that all this political activity was well-planned and orchestrated by those who have been the custodians of secret knowledge for thousands of years. Today they are called secret societies, and there are many of them in various forms and disguises. The Freemasons are possibly the most notorious, and their origins can be traced back for thousands of years. Some researchers, like William Bramley, believe that this connection could possibly be traced all the way to the garden of Eden and the Brotherhood of the Snake, which was possibly the first secret society ever formed consciously by a breakaway sector of humans.

All of this has been going on unbeknown to the rest of humanity, which continues to be manipulated by the same group of powerful people today. Our real human history is far more exciting and infinitely more mysterious than any Hollywood movie or Indiana Jones adventure. And yes . . . it is always about the gold.

So when I settled in this historically rich part of the world I had no clue that the stone ruins of South Africa would unlock the deep mystery of our ancient past and connect us to who we are today—on all levels—whether historically, genetically, or spiritually.

I began to walk the mountains in the entire region, exploring thousands of stone ruins and scratching my head about the meaning of it all. My journey took me to the far north of Botswana and the ancient serpent worship site of Tsodilo Hills, which is also known as the Mountain of the Gods—not a surprising name if we start listening to the wisdom of the African shaman. This site is also referred to as the "creation cave of the human race."

I explored the ruins in Zimbabwe—which include the highly confusing ruins at Great Zimbabwe—and many more strangely mysterious places. I call the Great Zimbabwe ruins confusing because that is what they are: anyone who tries to construct sense from mainstream academic literature about these ruins will not be able to. All you ever find is the same ill-informed academic rhetoric about how these stone structures are either just remains of kraals (cattle enclosures), or the remains of Bantu tribes of the past 200 to 400 years. No matter how hard you look there has been no serious attempt to connect this information to ancient cultures and advanced civilizations that predate anything we have encountered. And yet this was the message that I received very strongly from the stone ruins and Adam's Calendar. It was as if every day brought a new revelation, along with more clues and more evidence to help compile a cohesive storyline—one that would withstand the attacks of the establishment and deliver evidence of a vanished civilization with advanced knowledge and technology, deeply connected to the laws of nature and the ability to use the natural forces of Mother Earth to generate free energy.

I realized that there was a link between the mysterious Zimbabwe Birds and the ancient gold-mining activity all around southern Africa. It did not take long for me to establish that we are not dealing with a few hundred or even a few thousand ruins, but many more than we could ever have imagined—pointing to a vast vanished civilization about which we know absolutely nothing.

It was my unexpected meeting with Baba Credo Mutwa that solidified everything I was thinking and supported all my research and conclusions, no matter how strange they may have seemed. In this book we will explore these amazing stone structures, their underlying connections, and their meaning for humans today. More than just stones, they are temples. As you will see in later

■ *Tsodilo Hills, the Mountain of the Gods, in northern Botswana*

chapters, when looking at some of the structures with sacred geometry overlaid, they have strong messages of spirituality encoded in them. Additionally, it is no coincidence that these structures are made of stone—the most common material for temples. Finally, Adam's Calendar holds even more significance: it is the birthplace of humanity, and it is considered to be one of the two most sacred sites on Earth by the African shaman, confirmed by my meeting with Baba Credo Mutwa.

■ *Tsodilo Hills is also referred to as the "creation cave of the human race." The giant serpent that was worshipped is carved out of the bedrock on the left.*

Hidden History

THE QUEST FOR TRUTH about our human origins has led scholars and explorers down some fascinating paths. The past two centuries have seen giant leaps in scientific technology, which have allowed researchers to present some remarkable conclusions. It must be hastily added that most of what we have been presented so far about our human origins are only theories and hypotheses based on the latest information gathered by the messengers. It is a common mistake by people outside the areas of research to believe these theories to be the

■ *An Egyptian ankh carved into a glacier slab at Dreikopseiland, South Africa. This petroglyph is worth a thousand words: the ankh is inside a radiating circle, suggesting that the Lord of Light has the key to eternal life. It also suggests that the secret lies in the frequency of light or is linked to some kind of vibrational energy that combines sound and light. This knowledge would be consistent with the circular ruins of southern Africa that were used to generate energy by using sound and possibly also light. This understanding of the flow of energy in sound and light was rediscovered by Keely, Tesla, and Rife, among others, in the late nineteenth century.*

absolute final word on the subject. This process of misinformation often starts when the media get the facts all messed up, and before we know it, everybody believes it.

History has taught us that humans, and especially the appointed leaders of the establishment, do not take kindly to change and new information. All we have to do is look at some of the great discoveries of the past few centuries to realize how stubborn and arrogant we can be about our personal deep-seated belief systems. Many discoveries have been met with fierce resistance, especially by religious leaders and so-called scholars, who in reality should be promoting the concept of progress. Countless books have been written about the covering up of new discoveries because they did not fit the pretty picture held by authorities of the time. If you think that this is only how it happened in the past, and that today we are all well informed by the beloved media, you are not only incredibly naive but grossly mistaken.

■ *The ankh is one of the most recognized symbols of ancient Egypt. It represents the key to eternal life and knowledge.*

Think of Galileo, who was forced to retract his scientific findings about our solar system. He was placed under house arrest and tortured until he apologized and retracted his statements. It took about another 100 years for his theories to be accepted. Just cast your mind back to the first flight of the Wright brothers in 1903, which probably happened much earlier but could not be unleashed on the people of the time because the expert scientists of that era insisted that man could not fly a heavier-than-air machine. Consider the fantastic discoveries of Nikola Tesla and his free energy; Royal Raymond Rife, who found "the cure for all disease" and in 1931 demonstrated how to cure cancer at will in a laboratory. Around 1888 John Keely demonstrated his antigravity device: sound vibration machines that could drill stone of any density with absolute perfection, and even vibrational fields that could completely crush giant granite megaliths to the finest powder in just a few seconds. These discoveries were covered up so well that they were completely removed from the broader knowledge pool and remain so today.

Tesla, Rife, Keely, and many other lesser-known great minds of the past should have changed history dramatically, and yet they mysteriously faded into obscurity. During the course of exploration we are often presented with evidence and information outside our scope of comprehension—information that goes against everything we have been taught. This is, after all, what true science and discovery is all about: it has no limits, and it is forever changing. The only constant in science is "change." Our immediate knee-jerk response is often to reject new information because we have never heard about it before. I trust you will agree that this is not a scientific argument, and never will be.

Most of us know Albert Einstein as the genius who answered many of our questions about space-time and the speed of light. Like all true scientists,

Einstein himself pushed the boundaries of possibility. Very few of us are aware of the bulk of his work, or that one of his favorite subjects was called "spooky action at a distance." It basically shows how two particles separated by extreme distance and no connection between them of any nature still remain connected by some invisible force. When one of the particles is stimulated and responds in a specific way, the other particle also displays the same immediate response, across a vast distance, faster than the speed of light. This part of his research, which included the Philadelphia experiment in July 1943, has been very successfully ridiculed and covered up to a large extent.

Max Planck, the father of quantum physics, is another Nobel Prize winner who had a very advanced view of the universe, but whose "other" work is underplayed and derided. Planck was fascinated by the concept of the "matrix," which was an expression that emerged from the world of hardcore physics, not some Hollywood scriptwriter. He believed that the universe is connected by an invisible matrix—a grid of energy to which we are all connected through an invisible lattice of consciousness. Therefore, we all share a collective memory and knowledge that is held in this matrix—not in our brains.

In 1933 Paul Dirac won the Nobel Prize for physics when he showed that all matter in the universe originates from a source of gamma-ray light or energy. This matter emerges from the subatomic singularity state of nondual particles that eventually make up the whole universe and all the stuff in it. Researchers have shown that there are various forms of gamma-ray light, and some of this light crosses the whole universe in an instant, which could explain Einstein's

■ *Nikola Tesla*

■ *Royal Raymond Rife*

■ *John Worrell Keely—just like Tesla and Rife, he realized that sound is a prime creative source and that when truly understood, it can be used for most applications imaginable.*

spooky action at a distance. Gregg Braden is an American scientist and author who has done much research on this subject and published several highly informative books. What I find fascinating about this discovery is that it fits the long-held belief that the speed of light is actually not a barrier to travel, but the stuff that makes up light is the actual mechanism for traveling beyond the speed of light.

Tesla was another disenfranchised pioneer into the unseen, and he did thousands of experiments as part of his research. He showed that the Earth is "alive" with currents of energy that surface in various frequencies everywhere. He realized that this energy can be used to power any apparatus, and for any application conceivable. This energy did not need wires to be conducted; it was carried in the particles and molecules of air in a way that was not understood before. The Earth acted like a capacitor for this energy—an inexhaustible storage device that could provide any amount of energy needed anywhere. On the next page is an image of the Tesla Tower, from which Tesla beamed the free energy that could power people's homes and cars, without any wires. It is obvious that this kind of easy access to free energy was not well received by the controlling electricity giants. When his sponsor, J. P. Morgan, realized that this energy could not be measured or easily controlled, he stopped his funding of any future projects, demolished the tower, and the FBI confiscated all

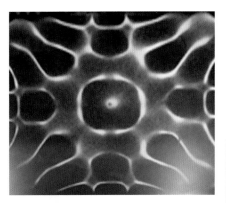

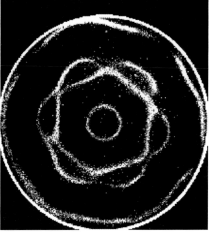

■ *This is the pattern created by the vibrational energy of the vowel "a." Notice the circle in the middle and that the outer circle is not perfectly round but has a wavelike shape around the perimeter.*

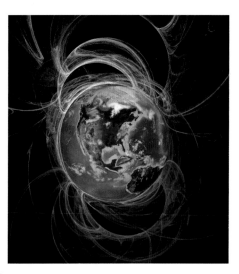

■ *Experiments at Harvard University show how sound energy creates patterns in sand. Low frequencies seem to create more basic circular patterns, while higher frequencies make more complex patterns. Interfering frequencies cause strange, complex patterns. The rule is quite simple— every frequency of energy manifests in a very unique pattern.*

■ *Computer-generated energy fields emanating from Earth all over its surface. This is what Tesla most likely tapped in to, to convert his free energy.*

documentation. Morgan ended up owning the giant hydroelectric power plants in North America. To this day no one has been able to emulate Tesla's free energy, and his methods remain a great mystery to all scientists. Tesla reportedly removed the engine from a convertible, replaced it with a black box of some sort, placed an aerial sticking out the backseat of the car, and drove the car around Long Island for about six weeks without any gasoline—just powered by the energy beamed from the Tesla Tower.

So as we explore the ancient stone ruins of South Africa and keep bumping into mysterious, inexplicable "stuff" and ponder its origins, we need to keep all of this in mind. We are uncovering vanished civilizations who had knowledge we can hardly imagine. We are knocking on the door of our human origins, and what we find is not always what we had expected. There are many questions

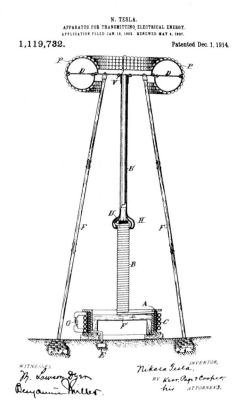

■ One of the hundreds of Tesla's patents. A device for transmitting electric energy— without wires. Note that Tesla called it radiant, nonpolar energy, not electricity. Therein lies a major clue for those who are trying to emulate his work.

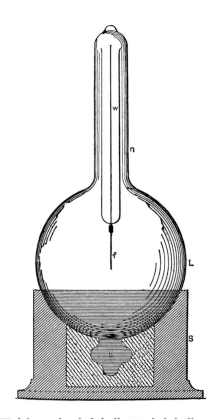

■ Tesla's wireless lightbulb. His lightbulb was just one example of tapping in to the Earth as an energy device. It had no wires and simply drew the energy from the hand of the person who held it. Some of the lightbulbs did not even need a touch from a person but simply lit up when a person was within close proximity.

■ *The Tesla Tower in Long Island, New York*

and only a few hypothetical answers based on our current pool of accumulated knowledge. I have been studying human origins for more than two decades, and there is only one conclusion that I have been able to reach in all this time: Things are not as they seem, and as soon as you begin to dig into the unknown past, you very quickly realize that hidden below the sands of time is a completely different history of humankind. We have a past that has somehow been hidden from view over thousands of years. The deeper we dig and the more we ask, the more convinced we become that what we have been told is not necessarily the absolute truth.

Human Origins
and Mythology

WHILE THE TRUE ORIGINS of humankind are still very murky and entangled in a never-ending tussle between evolutionists and creationists, there are fascinating clues left behind by ancient civilizations, and they point us in a very specific direction. All of this activity in the distant past cannot be separated from religion. Many ancient religious scripts that have survived from various corners of the world give us remarkable clarity on a multitude of issues. One such issue is the existence of a group of omnipresent gods and deities with advanced powers who seemed to have ruled the world for thousands of years. The Sumerian tablets called these gods the Anunnaki. Led by a mysterious pantheon of twelve gods, the Anunnaki—in various names—seem to be present in every ancient civilization, scattered across all the continents, separated by thousands of miles. In my research and books I make the intentional distinction between God with a capital "G" and god(s) with a lowercase "g." This highlights the difference between the true divine source of all things in the universe (God), and a group of advanced beings, the Anunnaki gods, who—though technologically advanced and the genetic progenitors of humankind—are not the creators of the universe and the source of all things and therefore cannot be confused with God. For more about this stunning history, see my book *Slave Species of the Gods*.

■ *The Caduceus—well known as the symbol of the medical profession. Its origin goes back thousands of years to the symbol of the Sumerian deity Enki, who was known as the winged serpent, or flying serpent. He was the creator of the human race and the god of medicine and healing. The winged serpent is worshipped by virtually every ancient civilization as their creator god, and serpent worship is associated with the creation of humans.*

Those who hold the Bible dear should not be surprised to find that these same deities and gods are referred to in the Bible on many occasions. In the original Bible, before it was translated and streamlined, the original word for *God* was *Elohim,* which is a plural word meaning "gods." This was always the case, and the biblical God has always been a plural—"the gods." Suddenly the many references by God to himself in the plural, like "Let us create man in our image" (Genesis 1:26) and "Let us go down and confuse their language" (Genesis 11:7) become less confusing.

When we realize that most of the stories from Genesis and Exodus are translations from their original source written in the Sumerian tablets, it all starts to make a lot more sense. The same gods that the Sumerian tablets refer to are the same plural Gods that are mentioned in the Bible. All the greatest biblical stories have their origins in the Sumerian tablets.

While the story is often reduced to one line in the Bible, the original Sumerian texts are written in much greater detail: The seven tablets of creation of heaven and Earth; creation of Adamu, the biblical Adam; creation of Eve from Adamu's rib; the garden of Eden; the serpent and the tree of knowledge and life; the Flood; Noah (Ziusudra) and the ark; destruction of Sodom and Gomorrah; the tower of Babel and its destruction by the gods, and many more. These tales are all well documented by the Sumerians, and some of these tablets predate the Bible by as much as 3,000 years.

It is also important to note that in Sumerian, Egyptian, Greek, and all other cultures, the gods are never considered imaginary but instead are very, very real. The Anunnaki interacted with the people, they informed the people, and they punished the people. The first so-called holy trinity arose in Sumeria. It was Anu—the father—and his two sons: Enlil and Enki. Together they ruled the roost on planet Earth. We know that Enlil was given the northern half of the planet to look after, and Enki—who was also known as the creator god, or serpent—was in charge of the southern part of the planet. They were supported by an extended family of a total of twelve central deities, each with special tasks and responsibilities. The Sumerian tablets refer to the sons of the Anunnaki as the Nephilim. Similarly, the Bible uses the term *Anakim* (giants), whose descendants are the Nephilim—who are also referred to as the "sons of the gods" in Genesis.

■ *Zeus fights his brother Hades for control of Earth. Hades is depicted as the winged serpent; he is banished to the underworld. This is also the story of the Sumerian deity brothers Enlil and Enki. Enlil took control of the upper world while Enki, the winged serpent, took control of the underworld. This was the land below the equator— where the gold came from. It was not hell, as it is often misinterpreted. Sumerians called this place ABZU.*

*The Nephilim were on the earth in those days—and also afterward—
when the sons of God [the gods] went to the daughters of men and had
children by them. They were the heroes of old, men of renown.*

GENESIS 6:4

This pantheon of ancient powerful gods or beings was also very active and very present in South Africa under their leader Enki. The evidence is everywhere, especially in the many references of the Sumerian tablets.

This leads us directly into one of the most misunderstood and misused expressions of our time: "mythology." This seemingly innocuous word has caused much confusion in our modern times and has caused us to completely misunderstand all of human history. The original meaning in Greek had nothing to do with "imaginary." In fact, it seems to be quite the opposite. The original meaning of *mythos* was "words": written words, spoken words, legend and tales of historic accounts sworn to be true by kings and priests.

Can you see the problem here? What was taken to be part of the daily life of ancient people has been reduced to imaginary fairy tales by modern historians. According to my research, it was around AD 1270 that the meaning of the word *mythological* was first misused and has subsequently created immense damage in all future history books.

Is it possible that all ancient civilizations never had a real history, real experiences, and real religion? Is it possible that they just imagined things because they could not understand the big bad world around them? This is exactly what some historians would like us to believe. Once we realize that *mythology* actually means "history," the whole picture changes quite dramatically. We suddenly realize that in the distant past there was a group of powerful beings (gods) who controlled events all over the planet, including southern Africa. This is instantly recognizable in the symbols and statues carved in rock in South Africa, which predate the Egyptian and Sumerian equivalents. It is important that the presence of these ancient so-called gods should not be confused with the true creator of the universe and all things in it—God.

Cornerstones
of Our Beliefs

■ *One of the many stone walls that still stands close to 3 meters high. A section of a large ruin with a diameter of 150 meters. A carved stone that resembles a human head stands close by, as if it were part of some kind of ritual. Many strange and inexplicable carved shapes of stone are found scattered among the ruins, accompanied by hundreds of unusual stone tools that were previously not recognized as such.*

THERE ARE THOUSANDS of religions and belief systems on Earth. Many are offshoots from ancient religions and belief systems. Christianity alone has more than 20,000 sects that all seem to have a slightly different take on the whole thing. I have identified three common denominators that are shared by all people, in every civilization on Earth as far back as we can push the envelope of human history. These commonalities are gold, slavery, and the feathered serpent, or winged/flying serpent. These are truly fascinating when analyzed in detail and cannot be separated from human history.

GOLD

No matter how far back in time we search, gold has always played a part in human activity. It was, however, not only humankind but also their gods who have been obsessed with gold. Even in the book of Genesis, God expresses his own obsession for this shiny metal. It makes no sense at all why ancient *Homo sapiens* and their creator would have been so consumed by gold, long before the appearance of currency or trade. For those who are keen to explore this further, I cover this subject and the real reasons for mankind's quest for gold in great detail in my book *Slave Species of the Gods*.

SLAVERY

Slavery has been practiced by mankind as far back as we can go. Even God's chosen people, according to the Bible, were enslaved by others. It is interesting to note that the ancient gods—which include the Gods of the Bible and Koran—not only condoned the practice of slavery but also gave the slave masters precise instructions on how to treat their slaves, how to punish their slaves, and under which circumstances they may kill their slaves. Why and how early humans stumbled upon the concept of slavery defies any logic but rather suggests that humankind was taught this unsavory activity by someone with a prior knowledge of it.

THE WINGED SERPENT

The winged or feathered serpent is regarded as the creator god in almost every ancient civilization. It was this so-called mythical creature who arrived out of the sky, created the people, gave them all their knowledge for survival, and punished them if they misbehaved. From the Sumerians to the Chinese, the North

Americans, Mesoamericans, and South Americans, South Africans to Egyptians serpent worship has always been a part of ancient civilizations.

Most of these tribes still use feathers in their traditional clothing and ritual dances, not realizing that this is actually a reference to the feathered serpent and their creator god from thousands of years ago. African culture is no different. Ancient Zulu tradition tells us of the Abelungu—great white sky gods, or "heaven dwellers," who once lived on Earth. They came from the blue sky on giant wings, and they could go back to heaven in a flash of light. They created the Zulu people and gave them life and knowledge, which included the working of gold.

These three common themes eventually wind together. It is truly curious that the symbol used by modern medicine today is the same ancient symbol used by the earliest Sumerian civilization to represent their creator god, the winged serpent Enki, who was also referred to as a medical master with knowledge of life and death and the caretaker of the first gold mines. By the time the greedy explorers from Europe arrived in southern Africa, the gold-mining civilization was already well developed and had been flourishing for thousands of years, but so was the dark practice of slavery. For at least five centuries before, Africa was well entrenched in this unsavory business, selling humans as property. According to experts the ports of Mozambique had exported large numbers of African slaves to the rest of the world. It seems that Africa has always been the inexhaustible source of slaves.

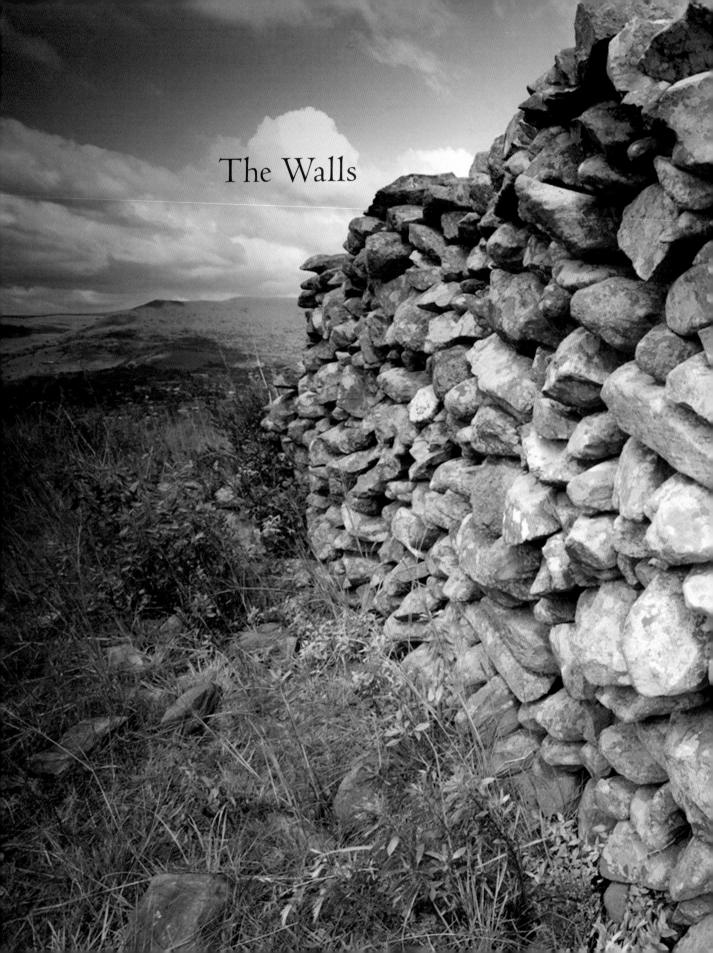

The Walls

■ One of the many thousands of dry stone walls that somehow survived are scattered throughout southern Africa. Until recently they were called kraals—of little historic importance. This widespread, ignorant perception by authorities has caused an unimaginable number of these ancient ruins to be destroyed by forestry, farming, and road works—destroying much crucial historic information with them.

THE FASCINATION WITH the ancient stone ruins in southern Africa goes back many centuries. Dozens of explorers—some of whom were simply greedy treasure hunters—have derived fame with their accounts of braving the savages of Africa to conquer the Dark Continent. In some social circles these stone ruins of the south have mesmerized explorers as much as the pyramids of Egypt. However, because Egypt is so often referred to as a great lost civilization, we often forget that Egypt is actually also in Africa. It is remarkable that, in essence, we are looking at two great civilizations at the opposite ends of the continent.

■ *We call this ruin the Stone Window. It sits high on a mountain, part of a large ruin. Because it faces east, the window is most likely an alignment for one of the solstices or equinoxes. It may also align with a specific star on the horizon—more research is necessary.*

Make no mistake, the discovery of this vanished civilization at the southern tip of Africa holds even more mystery than its northern cousin. It has more undeciphered mythology; countless stone ruins of unknown origin; great kings and wise men of the past; shamans and sangomas of the present who have upheld ancient tradition and preserved ancient knowledge; and most important, the same pantheon of gods who ruled all over the planet. The common links that we have identified leave no doubt that southern Africa did not escape the attention of the ancient gods. It is, however, very clear that the relationship those gods had with the ABZU (southern Africa) was quite different from their activities in other parts of the planet. It is very sad that we will never know the full extent of what existed at the most impressive ruins in southern Africa when they were first discovered by the colonialists from the north.

■ *Sections of walls in different ruins—some walls have thick lichen growing on them while others have moss, or both. There are a few different building styles indicating that they were built during earlier periods and altered by later arrivals. The oldest ones always display the same basic circular design— with no entrances.*

■ *From the grass among the ruins we have no idea that where we stand is part of a large complex on top of a mountain, which is linked by roads and other peculiar structures. Sometimes it is evident that the structures have been rebuilt by a more recent civilization and are not in their original form.*

The destruction and plundering that took place at these ruins will never be fully realized. It is certain that all valuable items were carted off by those who first found them, and not much consideration was given to their significance. Monoliths were removed and pushed aside without measuring their alignments with stars or their orientation to the cardinal points of Earth.

■ *Another stunning example of a wall that still stands 3 meters high. What cannot be seen from the ground is the road that runs into the structure. These stones come from a riverbed about 2 kilometers down the mountain.*

■ *Close-up of a small section of a wall indicating the large size of some of the stones. This large one weighs about 200–300 kilograms. Not the kind of stone you would want to carry up the mountain from the nearest river. So how and why did they go to so much trouble to do just that?*

■ *A good example of reconstruction by latter inhabitants who adapted the stone structure for their own needs—with doors and square shapes that indicate more recent usage. The rule is quite simple: when you see square structures, it means it was used by Westerners or European arrivals since the fifteenth century AD.*

■ *The author points out the height of the wall. This is one of the well-preserved ruins that was measured and found by Johan Heine to be aligned with many celestial aspects.*

■ *One of the many unexplained stones that are built into the walls. They were probably part of some ritual or alignment as yet not understood.*

■ *A spectacular effect of walls upon walls. This spectacular ruin near Waterval Boven was built from an estimated 500,000 stones—all brought up from the river in the valley. Current explanations are that this was built by a small family or two consisting of no more than fourteen people. Our calculation concludes that it would be impossible for such a small group of people to complete this structure in one lifetime.*

■ *The author crouches below a large rock that is part of a stone wall completely covered by soil. The entire complex is overgrown by trees and undergrowth; it cannot be seen from the ground by hikers, nor from a helicopter by those hunting for ruins—as he often does. He had to walk many mountains and crawl into many overgrown bush areas to truly discover the huge expanse of ruins that cover the landscape but remain invisible.*

■ *One of many mysterious circular passages surrounding a stone circle. It has no entrance nor exit—it simply ends in walls in all directions.*

■ The vast expanse of a ruined city near Rustenburg, South Africa. This is one of the three lost cities that I identified, covering about 10,000 square kilometers—larger than modern Johannesburg or Los Angeles. Its size makes it especially astounding that—like the other structures in southern Africa—all the stones used in this ancient city were not part of the natural bedrock but were transported to this site from the riverbed.

■ Outer wall of another ruin with several internal structures

■ *Examples of large stones in massive walls that are more than 1.5 meters wide, part of the lost city of Rustenburg. Some of these stones weigh well over 500 kilograms and were brought from a distance away—sometimes 3 kilometers or more.*

This was certainly the case at Mapungupwe—the most famous of the South African sites—where the one-horned golden rhino was discovered. Luckily, the golden rhino and other gold artifacts did survive. What was finally reported from these early sites is far from the truth, and we must not allow that information to skew our judgment.

During 2008 a very important event took place. The head of the University of Pretoria and several of their archaeologists were forced to apologize to the indigenous people of Limpopo for the desecration of Mapungupwe and various other sacred ancient sites. They promised to return most of the artifacts that were removed from the sites over the past sixty years or more;

■ *This is a great example of the high levels of destruction that some ruins exhibit. The large stones can be seen close to camera. For forces of nature to cause such high levels of decay, it would take a very long time and possibly some serious environmental disasters—such as a great flood. There is no reason or evidence to suggest that these structures were destroyed by other tribes.*

■ *A picture from 1939 shows a small hutlike structure completely constructed from stone slabs. The bottom picture shows the structure today with a collapsed roof. There is as yet no feasible explanation for the purpose of such a structure—all the obvious ones seem to apply our modern values and just don't fit any of our findings associated with these ancient civilizations. There are many of these very small circular stone enclosures in existence, and they all defy modern logic.*

■ *A view of a ruined wall in the foreground, and more ruined circles on the adjacent hill. The hills and mountains are covered with stone ruins. To the untrained eye they are mostly invisible, but examples like these are a good indicator of what this part of the world looked like many thousands of years ago.*

■ *Great Zimbabwe is no exception—walls in the foreground and ruined Acropolis on the hill in the distance. This mysterious ruin is part of the three lost cities we have discovered in southern Africa, and its structure is identical to the millions of other ruins. The grand entrance of Great Zimbabwe remains an awesome sight. (Photos by Bill Maliepaard)*

however, they were unable to account for many artifacts that had mysteriously vanished, such as a very large diamond that was among the items removed by archaeologists.

One of the first documented entries that describes large stone ruins in the fabled kingdom of Monomotapa—which would be central to northern Zimbabwe today—was made around AD 1512 by a Portuguese convict turned explorer named Antonio Fernandes. Even in Fernandes's time the stone structures were in ruin—completely overgrown and deserted. Fernandes was just one of many convicted criminals called *degradados* who were given the option to go to Africa to explore the dangerous Dark Continent for their European monarchs and report back on their findings . . . if they survived. It seems that the European kings and clergy of the time all had the same plan of action. They would send in the "great unwashed" to discover hidden treasures, only to send in the troops soon after to rape the land of all its wealth and enslave the natives. The early explorers caused death and destruction among the natives in all corners of the so-called New Worlds: the Americas, Africa, and India. This was all done in the name of God and greed, and always with the blessing of the pope.

In 1552 Fernandes's successor Joao de Barros wrote about large mysterious stone ruins. He also described a lintel above the entrance with inscriptions that could not be deciphered, even by the learned Moors who knew many languages. What is really curious about this event is that these Moorish wise men could not even identify the script, which was carved into the lintel. Sadly, this precious lintel has long since mysteriously disappeared. It is important to remember that the local tribes did not have a written language at this time in history, and yet there were inscriptions on these ruins. From the written entries it is clear that de Barros and the Moors knew with certainty that these ruins were there for the purpose of extracting gold. According to Roger Summers in *Ancient Ruins and Vanished Civilizations of Southern Africa,* when de Barros asked the local tribes of the area about the original builders, he was told that it must have been built by the devil, because "it does not seem possible that they should be the work of man."

Modern historians and academics have rushed to place a date on the building of these stone structures and automatically assume that the ruins must have been built by the people living in the area, or perhaps by their immediate ancestors. I would assume that if the ancestors of the local populations could write, these populations would have retained such a precious ability. This was not the case, however.

■ *Section of a large ruin overlooking adjacent hills. As far as you can see, the hills were once covered with structures like these.*

The migration of the Bantu people from the north into this region of southern Africa—especially Zimbabwe, and later into South Africa—remains a hotly debated subject. While some claim that this event can be traced to around the year 0, others argue it cannot be traced further back than about AD 1200. For many years it has been suggested that the arrival of the Bantu—and later the Europeans—caused the demise of the Khoisan,* who

---

*The term *Khoisan* (previously Bushmen) is a general term for two ethnic groups: the pastoral Khoi and the foraging San.

were driven from their ancestral lands. These theories keep changing and have changed again in the past few years. It is now speculated that the Khoi arrived in South Africa from eastern Africa around 2,000 years ago. Therefore, it is argued that many or most of the rock engravings associated with this group cannot be older than 2,000 years.

This is just another silly example of the reverse application of logic. In science we cannot force the evidence to fit our theories, and yet this is what I keep stumbling upon in my research as an independent scientist. Our theories should be formulated from the evidence we find. Any seasoned archaeologist should be able to determine from the erosion that the so-called Khoisan petroglyphs are many thousands of years old simply by observing the cracks that have formed through them.

These theories about the arrival of the Bantu and Khoi people from the north suggest that southern Africa was an empty land until they arrived here. Yet millions of stone tools have been discovered, and many more lie beneath the sand. How many *Homo erectus* or *Homo habilis* lived here in ancient times to have needed all these millions of tools? Countless ruined stone dwellings lie scattered throughout the lands without any attention from academics. It is time for our historians to wake up and face reality—deal with the evidence and not just conveniently shove it under the carpet.

Current history books and government papers categorically state that South Africa was very sparsely populated by small groups of migrating people from the north until the early 1700s. There is still much debate about the events surrounding the migration of the early settlers into southern Africa; details surrounding the arrival of Bantu people, the Khoi, and the San are still very speculative. Some scholars continue to insist that the stone structures of Zimbabwe and South Africa could not have been built before the settlement of the Bantu people in this part of Africa. This is another clear case of forcing the data to fit the existing theory despite being surrounded by the evidence of an earlier, vanished African civilization.

The mainstream scientific community continues to tout this narrative, with no thought to the existence of the massive, mysterious structures all around. To highlight this confusion, I insert an extract from the South African Government Info website (www.gov.za). According to this information, though "modern humans" have lived in this region for "over 100,000 years," the Khoi and the San have been present in southern Africa for as little as 2,000 years.

■ *Part of a mud hut wall remains inside a large stone circle. Clear indication how later arrivals adapted the ruins for their own needs. Many examples like this have been found. This has caused some scholars to believe that the circular stone structures were built by the same people who then constructed the mud huts inside. No evidence to support such theories has been produced. What these discoveries show is proof of habitation of recent occupants—not proof of constructions of the original stone structure.*

■ *Part of a Stone Age structure with a flat stone altar against one of the walls. Several tools from the Middle Stone Age have been found here.*

■ *Small section of a very different style of wall building, using mud as mortar between the stones. This lies about 30 meters from the ruin above, showing once again how civilizations build on top of each other, reusing the materials from the previous inhabitants.*

The Early Inhabitants

The discovery of the skull of a Taung child in 1924; discoveries of hominid fossils at Sterkfontein caves, a world heritage site; and the ground-breaking work done at Blombos Cave in the southern Cape, have all put South Africa at the forefront of palaeontological research into the origins of humanity. Modern humans have lived in the region for over 100,000 years.

The small, mobile bands of Stone-Age hunter-gatherers, who created a wealth of rock art, were the ancestors of the Khoikhoi and San of historical times. The Khoikhoi and San . . . although collectively known as the Khoisan, are often thought of as distinct peoples.

The former were those who, some 2,000 years ago, adopted a pastoralist lifestyle herding sheep and later, cattle. Whereas the hunter-gatherers adapted to local environments and were scattered across the subcontinent, the herders sought out the pasturelands between modern-day Namibia and the Eastern Cape, which, generally, are near the coast. At around the same time, Bantu-speaking agropastoralists began arriving in southern Africa, bringing with them an iron-age culture and domesticated crops. After establishing themselves in the well-watered eastern coastal region of southern Africa, these farmers spread out across the interior plateau, or "Highveld," where they adopted a more extensive cattle-farming culture.

The mystery of the stone ruins lingers. The inexplicable elements are the large numbers of ruins and settlements, the sheer size of the area they cover, the hundreds of kilometers of ancient roads, thousands of large stone monoliths and statues aligned to many celestial and geographic elements, thousands of kilometers of agricultural terraces, and the size of the population required to have built all these structures.

From the accounts of Joao de Barros it is much more feasible that the mysterious inscription at Great Zimbabwe was not the work of the new African settlers from the north—who most likely just occupied the structure—but an earlier southern African civilization, who were well evolved in the art of building with stone and, more important, a people who had the knowledge of writing.

Obsession with the Stars

VIRTUALLY ALL ANCIENT civilizations were obsessed with the stars. They observed them, they worshipped them, they tracked their movement, they depicted them in art and rock engravings, and they carved images of celestial beings from stone. Their knowledge of the cosmos was astounding. The Maya from Mesoamerica are possibly the best example of this with their variety of precise calendars, which can measure time and cosmic events for millions of years into the past and the future. They knew about the 26,000-year precessional wobble of planet Earth, and their Long Count calendar is based on this time period. They also knew that the constellations of Scorpio and Sagittarius point to the center of our galaxy: the Milky Way. It was only in the latter part of the twentieth century that scientists began to realize that these ancient people had a much more advanced knowledge of the cosmos than we have, and more scientists are joining this group of believers on a daily basis.

The most frequent star systems linked with life on Earth are Sirius, the Pleiades, and Orion's Belt. While Orion played a major part in the alignments and construction of the Giza pyramids, the Mayan pyramids, the Chinese pyramids, and even Great Zimbabwe, it is Sirius that has caused many surprises. Sirius is also the key star in the construction of the Great Pyramid, while the Egyptian Sothic calendar is based on it as well. The second of the two southern shafts of the Great Pyramid points to Orion. It is believed that these shafts represent the ascension of the pharaoh's soul to the source of life, which was believed to be Orion and Sirius. This is just a tiny taste of the vast ancient knowledge of the cosmos.

If you think that this advanced knowledge of the cosmos was not present among the ancient tribes of southern Africa, you are grossly mistaken. This obsession is deeply entrenched in ancient southern African tradition. According to Credo Mutwa there are various "star tribes" in Africa who carry great star knowledge. The Ndebele people are the ones who carry the ancient knowledge of the Mbube star of Orion—the Far-walking Constellation, or Umhabi. Johan Heine's meticulous exploratory work at Adam's Calendar has shown that these ancient civilizations in the south were in touch with the stars long before anyone

Orion
Betelgeuse
Belatrix
Alniltak
Alnitam
Mintaka
Pyramid alignm...
Winter solstice
WEST

■ A three-dimensional reconstruction of Adam's Calendar showing the Horus statue and three Orion stones—aligned perfectly to the rise of Orion's belt on the vernal equinox, when it was flat on the horizon. Current calculations indicate that this would have occurred at least 160,000 years ago. More measurements and calculations are necessary.

■ Sirius A with its tiny binary partner, Sirius B, to the bottom left

else. While our first calculations showed Adam's Calendar has been aligned with the rise of Orion's Belt on the spring equinox some 75,000 years ago, the latest calculations point to a date well over 160,000 years ago. Much more measuring needs to be done, and I am certain that we will find a clear link to Sirius very soon, for the simple reason that Credo Mutwa suggests that life on Earth originated from the Sirius planetary system. And so far he has not been wrong about much.

The Dogon people of Mali are another African star tribe who show an uncanny knowledge of cosmic affairs. The Dogon belief, which has been part of their custom for thousands of years, is that life on Earth came from Sirius. They have always known that the brightest star in the sky, Sirius, has a twin, Sirius B. They also knew that our sun was actually part of the Sirius binary system, as a third star. This has also only very recently become known to a small enlightened group of astrophysicists, as described by American researcher Walter Cruttenden in his book *Lost Star of Myth and Time*. The Dogon priests claimed that Sirius had a companion star, which was invisible to the human eye. They also said that the star moved in a fifty-year elliptical orbit around Sirius. They said that it rotated on its axis, that it was small and white, and that it was the "heaviest star."

This information was only discovered by modern astronomers as recently as 1844, when they began to suspect that Sirius A had a companion star. They noticed that the path of the star was irregular and wobbly, which would suggest a second star present. In 1862 Alvan Clark discovered the second star, confirming the hypothesis that Sirius was indeed a binary star system. In the 1920s it was determined that Sirius B was a white dwarf star, smaller than planet Earth. White dwarfs are dense stars that burn dimly with an extremely high gravity. It is this gravitational pull that causes the wobbly, wavy movement of Sirius A. The Dogon name for Sirius B is Po Tolo, which can be translated as "smallest seed"—*Po;* and "star"—*Tolo.* The "seed" refers to creation and the seeding of Earth from Sirius.

For thousands of years the Dogon have attributed three principal properties to Sirius B: small, heavy, white. This is not something we can conveniently explain away, as scholars often prefer to do because they do not want to deal with the mystery. We have to be sober about this and attempt to get to the true origins of this knowledge pool. How could this seemingly primitive tribe from Africa have possibly known this?

Once we start to analyze the millions of stone ruins of southern Africa it becomes evident that the ancient builders had a very good knowledge of the cosmos themselves. One of the most compelling features of many of the larger

stone ruins is that they are aligned with the cardinal points of Earth, solstices, equinoxes, and most likely Sirius, Orion, and other key stars also. Johan Heine was the first real pioneer in this field who measured and analyzed more ruins than anyone else and, by doing so, exposed the ancient skills of the FIRST architects.

Many ruins display very complex geometric forms and the knowledge of advanced geometry. This includes the phi factor (φ), or golden ratio of approximately 1.618, which is the factor by which nature and space arranges itself. Examples of this divine plan can be seen in the shape of seashells, pinecones, the proportion of the human body, and all living matter on Earth or in the cosmos—even the way galaxies arrange themselves. It is also referred to as the golden mean spiral and is linked to the free flow of energy in nature and the universe. This ancient knowledge is evident in the construction of Adam's Calendar, which is also linked to the pyramids in the valley below

■ *Eastern view of a three-dimensional reconstruction of Adam's Calendar. The oldest version of the Egyptian Horus hawk stands in line with the spring equinox sunrise. To the right are the three aligned stones of Orion. Farther up in the top right corner you can see the faint outline of the two pyramids also aligned with Orion's rise. The pyramids are directly aligned with Great Zimbabwe and the Great Pyramid of Giza in Egypt, along 31 degrees east longitude.*

■ *A spiral galaxy as an example showing how everything in nature conforms to the Golden Mean spiral, or phi ratio, of 1.618.*

by a golden mean spiral. The probability that this connection is accidental is outweighed by several million to one; there must be a conscious link between the two sites.

Many scholars have ascribed the construction of the stone ruins to the migrating hunter-gatherers and agrarians from the early Iron Age some 2,000 years ago and later to the Bantu tribes from the eighteenth century AD. No evidence can be found that these people built their structures with such precise alignments. This was certainly not the custom among the early settlers from the north but rather something much more mysterious left behind by a vanished ancient African civilization of the south—the ancestors of them all—the FIRST people.

When Cyril Hromnik wrote his masterpiece, *Indo-Africa,* in 1981, he made many enemies with his outlandish suggestions that much of South Africa's current culture was influenced by Indians, specifically the Dravidian ethnic group from southern India. His impeccable research in this area leaves little doubt that there was a large presence of Dravidian gold miners and merchants over an extended period as far back as 2,000 years ago and possibly even earlier. They left behind an unmistakable range of influence, which is evident in many aspects of South African culture and indigenous languages. Many of the stone ruins I have explored can be linked directly to the Dravidian culture, on which Hromnik has written many papers.

The Dravidians left behind some important clues and even names that we still use in South Africa today. As Hromnik states in his 1996 paper:

Until the 16th century the gold producing region of Mpumalanga was known as "Komatiland." Early Portuguese sources describe it as Terra dos Macomates, the land of the Komati people. Komati, was the professional name of a Dravidian merchant caste of South India. This name is still attached to the Komati River, Komatipoort, etc. During centuries of gold exploration they mixed with the indigenous Kung (Bushmen) creating the Quena (Otentottu), and with the Black people from the NW creating the aBantu people, and together they gave rise to the MaKomati. The pre-European form of the name was MaKomatidesa, Land of the MaKomati.

It is evident that many of the circular stone settlements I have explored are the remains of the Dravidians, who were obsessed with observing the movement of the sun and other celestial activities. Hromnik's detailed study of the Chariot of the Dying Sun ruin near Carolina in Mpumalanga is a great example of this. An aerial photo of this ruin is on this page 58. Many alignments of monoliths, shrines, and other marker stones seem to be the work of these gold merchants from Asia. These precise alignments to the movement of the sun were intended by its Dravidian architects probably more than 1,000 years ago. However, it is possible that this structure was originally designed many thousands of years earlier by the FIRST people, who were the ancestors of all others on Earth, including the Dravidians. By the time the Dravidians arrived here some 2,000 years ago, they would have recognized many of the original symbols and structures aligned to the same celestial bodies they were accustomed to. They simply needed to fine-tune the ruins for their own needs. From my perspective this structure displays the same circular configurations consistent with harmonic-resonant chambers and energy-generating structures. The alignments to the sun were probably an important aspect of the design but not necessarily the primary objective. The creation of energy seems to be the main design objective in most of the circular ruined structures. This topic will be discussed in more detail in the chapter "Shapes of Ruins as Energy Devices," page 116.

There are dozens of examples of shrines scattered throughout Mpumalanga, and many of these show Dravidian symbols and shapes. It is important to point out, however, that thousands of petroglyphs carved into rock also link people from southern Africa to other ancient cultures besides the Dravidians, especially the Sumerians and Egyptians. This follows our logic and argument, because

■ *Chariot of the Dying Sun ruin*

there simply were not enough Dravidian miners in southern Africa to have built millions of stone structures.

It seems to me that—irrespective of the evidence that the earliest humans on Earth lived in this part of the world and developed the first art, first community, first mining, and the first cities on Earth—some scholars truly believe that southern Africa was a vacant piece of land with no history until the migration south of the settlers from the north—black and white. We need to remind ourselves of the first rule of archaeology: civilizations build on top of each other. Even in modern cities like London and Rome archaeologists are discovering older layers deep below the surface, exposing a hidden past. For now we can only imagine the mysteries of the lost civilizations scattered throughout southern Africa below the layers of sand. But what caused those ancient cities to be covered by soil in such large numbers? I will discuss one possible reason—a global catastrophe—in the upcoming chapter, "The Flood," page 79.

■ *Johan Heine measuring and decoding another stone ruin to identify its celestial alignments and structural meaning.*

Adam's Calendar

■ *A graphic view of the central calendar stones at Adam's Calendar. The taller stone's carved edge allows the shadow of the setting sun on the winter solstice to reach the edge of the second flat stone.*

■ *The stone altar, possible resting place of the Sumerian deity Dumuzi. The image below demonstrates the energetic results of dowsing at the altar.*

CREDO MUTWA CALLS Adam's Calendar the most sacred site on Earth, where Heaven mated with Mother Earth. It is also called Inzalo ye Langa in Zulu, meaning "birthplace of the sun." African knowledge keepers believe that this is the place where the gods created the first humans. Baba Credo was initiated here in 1937. Adam's Calendar is a well-known sacred site among sangomas and shamans. Many references in the Sumerian tablets describe how Enki built himself a special place of observation in the deep ABZU. It was on the edge of a cliff, in line with his abode farther north—which I believe was Great Zimbabwe—and the Great Pyramids in Egypt, which are referred to as the "twin peaks." (This reference to the pyramids may, however, be a reference to the mysterious pyramids in the valley below. Because at the time of the construction of Adam's Calendar the Giza pyramids were most likely not yet constructed.) There is no other place that matches this description better than Adam's Calendar—a special place of observation. All the evidence leads me to this conclusion. On a more spiritual note, many psychics have told me independently that it is indeed a place built by Enki. On a

■ *Adam's Calendar in three dimensions. All the calendar stones are dolerite, while the bedrock is black reef quartzite. It is the edge of what is known as the Transvaal escarpment. All the calendar monoliths were brought from some distance away to be shaped and erected.*

■ *The statue of the Horus Hawk*

television special, on the Afrikaans channel Kyknet, that exposed sacred places in South Africa, a psychic exposed that this was the oldest place on Earth and that it was built even before humans existed.

The stories and stones of Adam's Calendar tell tales that are not told in the history books. They connect the FIRST people of southern Africa to the Egyptian civilization. This site contains the first statue of the Horus Hawk, which was made famous through Egyptology. This statue is probably well over 200,000 years old. Our calculations of Orion's Belt alignments seem to be leaning in that direction. Note the broken nose or beak of the Horus bird lying flat on the side of the mountain. This staggering age of this statue is evidence that the Egyptians inherited much of their core symbols from the FIRST people in southern Africa.

■ *Sunrise over the stones; one of multitudes, with no end in sight*

Adding to the site's singular history, there is an extraordinary stone altar about 700 meters north of Adam's Calendar. Various energy measurements and infrared photography suggest that it is a grave. The Sumerian tablets often refer to Inanna and Dumuzi; they were the Sumerian Romeo and Juliet. We read that the Sumerian deity Dumuzi was buried in the deep ABZU, on the edge of a cliff on top of a mountain facing east, at his father's special place. His father was the Sumerian deity Enki. This may yet become one of the most important historic discoveries linking human prehistory and so-called mythology to the twenty-first century.

South African Sphinx

THE FIRST SPHINX statue stands proudly near the ritual path at Adam's Calendar. A recent discovery, it is another crucial clue about the origins of the most important symbols in human history. As was suggested by the Horus Hawk in the previous chapter, these symbols did not originate in Egypt or Sumeria but in South Africa. This may also be the site of the first large statue of Inana, the Sumerian deity often discussed in the tablets. The tablets recollect her love for the ABZU, so it is fitting she be immortalized in these stones. This site is still extremely powerful and continues to be used for initiations.

■ *The Sphinx*

■ *A good view of the ritual path at Adam's Calendar that joins the northern site to the main calendar site. The path runs among hundreds of fallen dolerite monoliths that all show signs of carving and shaping like the monolith in the picture to the right. This is a great example of unfinished work by ancient craftsmen.*

■ *A statue of Inanna in the Paris museum. She is depicted standing on two African gazelle, indicating her dominion over the ABZU*

■ *One of the many Sumerian tablets that refer to Inanna in the ABZU (Courtesy of the University of Pennsylvania Museum of Archaeology and Anthropology)*

■ *A headless statue along the ritual path at Adam's Calendar. It is possibly the first large statue of Inanna.*

■ *The Sphinx statue from a different angle*

■ *A view of Adam's Calendar from the south—perched on the edge of the cliff looking east toward the two pyramids and the rising sun on the spring equinox.*

■ *The Skull stone. One of the many monoliths that show signs of severe erosion. Geologists agree that this kind of erosion would take many hundreds of thousands of years to occur. This one eroded much faster because it was part of the ritual initiation ceremony outlined to me by Credo Mutwa. The initiates were required to urinate on this stone. Nevertheless, erosion of the dolerite stones is a good indicator of the real age of the site.*

Adam's Pyramids

■ *Adam's Pyramids visible behind golden grasses*

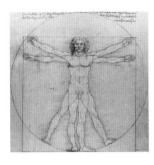

■ *Da Vinci's* Vitruvian Man

ARCHITECTS AND ARTISTS over the centuries—up to the present day—have copied their ancient ancestors by applying the Golden Mean spiral into their grand, modern constructions and art. Leonardo da Vinci's *Vitruvian Man* is one of the best examples of this—and points directly to secret knowledge held by da Vinci himself. It seems that Dan Brown was spot on with his book *The Da Vinci Code*. When we think of pyramids we immediately imagine the spectacular pyramids of Giza or the Mayan pyramids, both of which are built from giant blocks of stone. They take our breath away each time we see them. These, however, are the exception to the rule. Most pyramids do not look like that. Hundreds of

■ *Adam's Pyramids as seen from the calendar site on the edge of the escarpment. They are about 11 kilometers away in the Barberton impact crater, which is about three billion years old and is the home of the oldest rock formations on Earth. It may not be a coincidence that Sheba Gold Mine is about 2 kilometers away from the pyramids.*

■ *A Golden Mean spiral perfectly links Adam's Calendar, the stone altar just north of it, and the two pyramids in the valley. This cannot be a coincidence. Because of this spiral there can be no doubt that these structures were erected in their positions for very specific reasons, which must include the flow of energy.*

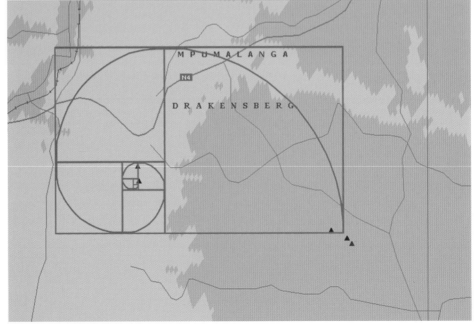

pyramids around the world are reduced to piles of rubble that simply approximate the shapes of a pyramid. This does not mean that they are not pyramids, and most of the pyramids in Egypt are of the lesser category.

In 2008 I accidentally discovered two pyramids in the valley below Adam's Calendar. At first I could not believe my eyes—I dismissed them as hills that simply looked like pyramids. But curiosity got the better of me when I realized that virtually every point at the calendar site is aligned or linked to the pyramids in some way. After all, the Egyptians built Sphinxes, Horus statues, and pyramids. We had already discovered a Sphinx and a Horus statue, so why not pyramids?

After inspecting the mountainous outcrop lines in the valley I confirmed that the pyramid mounds are not part of the rock outcrop forming concentric rings that protrude from the center of the impact crater. These two mounds are much larger, slightly out of line with the concentric bedrock, and perfectly aligned to the rise of Orion's Belt from the center of Adam's Calendar. Some time prior to this I discovered that the Great Pyramid, Great Zimbabwe, and Adam's Calendar are all aligned along the 31 degree east longitudinal line. But

■ Johan Heine in 2003. This photograph clearly shows the pyramids in the distance shortly after he discovered the calendar. He began measuring and observing the movement of the sun. It took another seven years for me to notice the pyramids in the valley below perfectly aligned with Orion's rising.

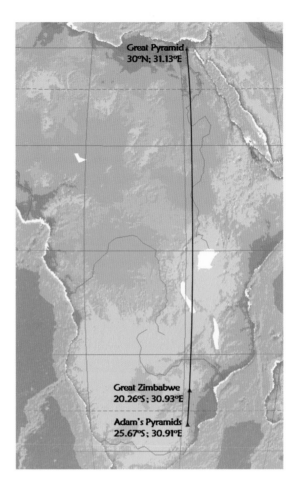

■ *A perfectly straight line along the 31 degree east longitude joins Adam's Pyramids, Great Zimbabwe, and the Great Pyramid of Giza. This is an intentional arrangement to facilitate the flow and harnessing of energy. This longitudinal line is also called the Nilotic Meridian and is associated with the sacred white lions of Timbavati. This line was an important ancient link to the galactic core—or the Great Sun as referred to by the ancients.*

Adam's Calendar is slightly out of line, to the left, if the line was drawn connecting the three sites from north to south.

Could it be that Adam's Calendar was somehow linked to the pyramids in the valley? I was convinced that there had to be a significant link between the two major points on the cliffs of the calendar and the pyramids some 11 kilometers away, otherwise all this activity and construction along the cliff would have made very little sense. In hindsight I should have guessed this immediately. The monoliths at the center of Adam's Calendar, the stone altar north of it, and the pyramids are perfectly connected by a Golden Mean spiral. And so it is not Adam's Calendar that is directly in line with the ruins at Great Zimbabwe and the Giza Pyramids, but rather the pyramids of Adam's Calendar that are perfectly aligned. It now seems that just like the Great Pyramid was said to have been the energy source of ancient Egypt, Adam's Pyramids were the energy source for the calendar and other sites not yet discovered.

Measurements

■ *The Hexagon: carefully constructed with sacred and scientific knowledge.*

THE RUIN WE call the Hexagon is one of the most important Johan Heine has discovered and measured. The structure and alignments suggest an advanced knowledge of the cosmos, geometry, and particle physics. It is molded around the structure of a star tetrahedron, which is referred to by leading scientists as the fundamental structure of all matter in the universe. It is also synonymous with what the ancients called the fruit of life.

In the image on this page we can also see the continuous repetition of star tetrahedrons inward. Therefore, it is a good example of infinity within a finite space in physics and geometry. Take note that the star of David is actually a flattened representation of a star tetrahedron, indicating ancient sacred knowledge. It is not really a religious symbol, which it became in later years for all the wrong reasons. Notice the six circles that surround the one in the center—six around one. This is referred to as the creation event in sacred geometry.

■ *The Hexagon, with star tetrahedron overlay.*

■ *A diagram of the fruit of life and its relationship to a star tetrahedron.*

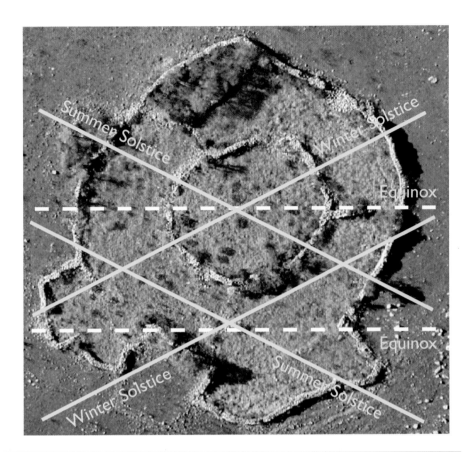

■ *The alignments of the Hexagon suggest an advanced knowledge of the cosmos.*

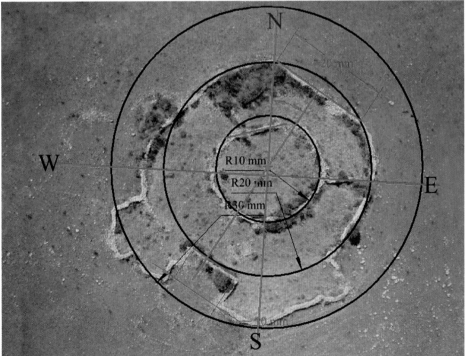

■ *The concentric circles in the structure indicate knowledge of quantum physics and generation of energy through resonant chambers.*

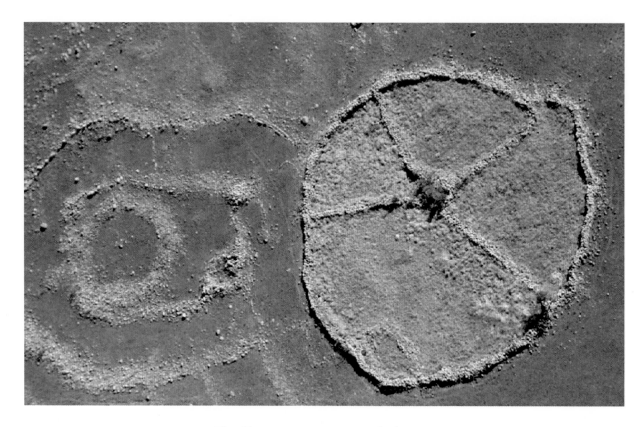

■ *The Chromosome, or Wagon Wheel ruin.*
Shown also with cardinal points overlay.

Another structure demonstrating advanced knowledge is the Chromosome, or Wagon Wheel. It is also clearly aligned to important cardinal points, but its relationship to the surrounding ruined structures is even more impressive. The distinct horseshoe shape, or ohm shape (Ω), to the left of the circular structure clearly played an important role in its original function. The ohm shape is synonymous with sound and chanting. (The *om* sound is the most commonly made sound in chanting. The *mmmm* causes resonance between the lips, making the chanter acutely aware of its physical effects.) The smaller circle inside the ohm shape leaves no doubt that sound was utilized for some purpose. It suggests that this structure was important in the generation of sound frequency. There are many such ohm shape ruins scattered across the region.

Probably the most complex of the ruins, the Phi Factor shows a great understanding and mastery of geometry. It was clearly constructed with knowledge of the Golden Mean ratio and phi. It also supports the Hexagon and star tetrahedron structure. We need to do much more work to get closer to understanding these complex designs. We cannot apply our current way of thinking to them. They originate from a completely different time and a civilization that did not think the way we do today. It remains the biggest mystery in our human history.

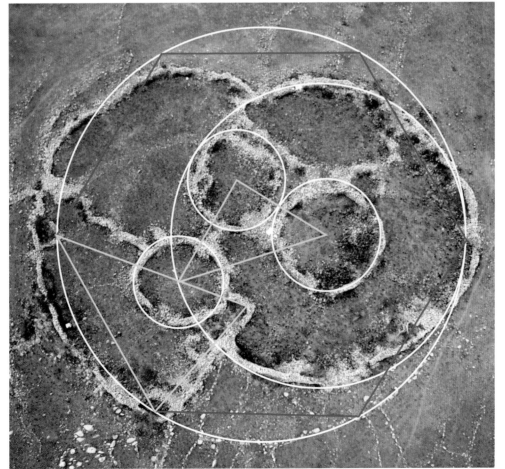

■ *The Phi Factor ruin. The outside wall has long gone, but faint traces of it can still be seen to fit the large circle.*

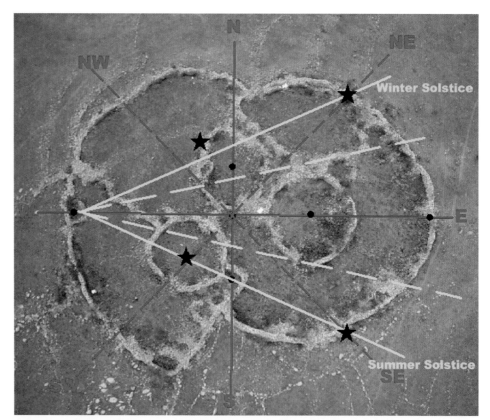

■ *Johan Heine's meticulous research over fifteen years provides irrefutable evidence that the ruins were constructed with intent and awareness of the cardinal points of planet Earth and deeply rooted knowledge of sacred geometry. It indicates a high level of intelligence and ability not recognized by historians in South Africa to date.*

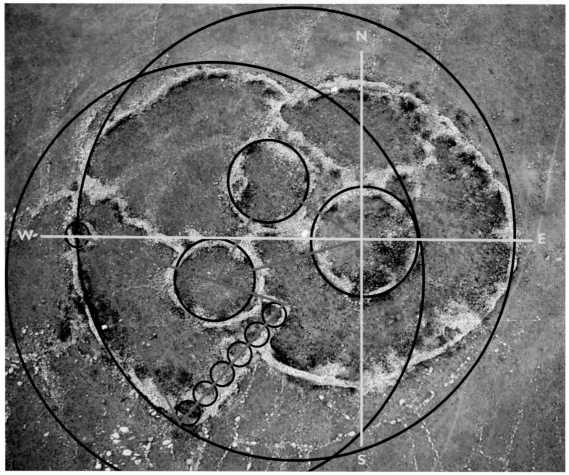

The Flood

MOST PEOPLE ARE familiar with the biblical Flood. Some believe that it was just a story with no real relevance in human history. Well, this is not so. The Great Flood, or Deluge, as it is referred to by historians, actually did happen. This event took place around 12,000 to 13,000 years ago, based on various archaeological discoveries. Many scholars attribute such an event to the rather sudden end of the last ice age, but there are many that claim the Flood happened for entirely different reasons.

In his book *Genesis of the Cosmos,* Dr. Paul LaViolette found evidence in core samples of polar ice that there was such a catastrophic event as far back as 14,500 years. His research focuses on the volatile nature of the galactic bulge—the center of our galaxy—which produces vast, regular supernova-like explosions. The intervals at which these central galactic explosions occur correlate with what ancients called the appearance of the "Blue Star"—which preceded the disastrous collapse of civilizations. The Maya believed that approximately 5,200 years constitutes an "age" of humanity, after which the people on Earth are destroyed to give rise to a new age. Such new civilizations have to figure out that they were not the first advanced people on this planet but were preceded by many others who lived very different lives in different social structures with different values. The Maya called these destruction and construction cycles—which LaViolette would later describe—the "five ages," and it was one of these events that caused the Great Flood.

The Sumerian tablets give us a graphic description—which is consistent with the Mayan prophecies and LaViolette's work—of the events that led to the Great Flood. The Great Flood was also the trigger point for many advanced civilizations to suddenly emerge in multiple locations around the world. We are told that the entire ice sheet layer that covered Antarctica slipped into the ocean, causing a spectacular cascade of gigantic waves pounding the whole planet. The waves would have been several kilometers high, traveling at close to 1,000 kilometers per hour—like a ring of water around the planet—speeding from the South Pole toward the North Pole, annihilating everything in its path. The ice

■ *Halfway up a mountain near Lydenburg, a new road exposes 3 meters of sediment that show stones from ruined walls and thousands of stone tools of an anomalous kind. This is a good argument for the theory that the Flood destroyed the FIRST civilization and covered their stone structures by soil.*

sheet slid because a large celestial body entered the solar system and came so close to Earth's orbit that it caused huge geophysical disturbances—more than the Earth had experienced in human history. The gravitational effect on Earth was so large that it caused the glacial ice sheets, which were already weakened by the rising global temperatures, to slide into the oceans.

The countries closest to the source of the tidal waves would have been completely devastated: South America, Australia, New Zealand, and southern Africa. While some ancient ruins on top of mountains remained standing, everything else would have been overrun by the waters and covered by soil and sand. That is why the majority of stone ruins of the ancient southern African civilization lie below the soil but remain visible to the trained eye. I believe that the structures we see today are those that were rebuilt in much smaller quantities by the survivors who reseeded the postdiluvian civilizations that rose again after the Flood. The evidence just cannot be dismissed as anything else. All the civilizations that emerged after the Flood did so with a whole new vigor and new knowledge, which they had to have acquired somewhere. They all shared a common obsession to accumulate more gold than they had ever done before. In the chapter titled "Ancient Levitation Device and White Powder of Gold," (page 112) I will discuss some reasons why gold was such a vital commodity.

Lost Cities—Vanished Civilizations

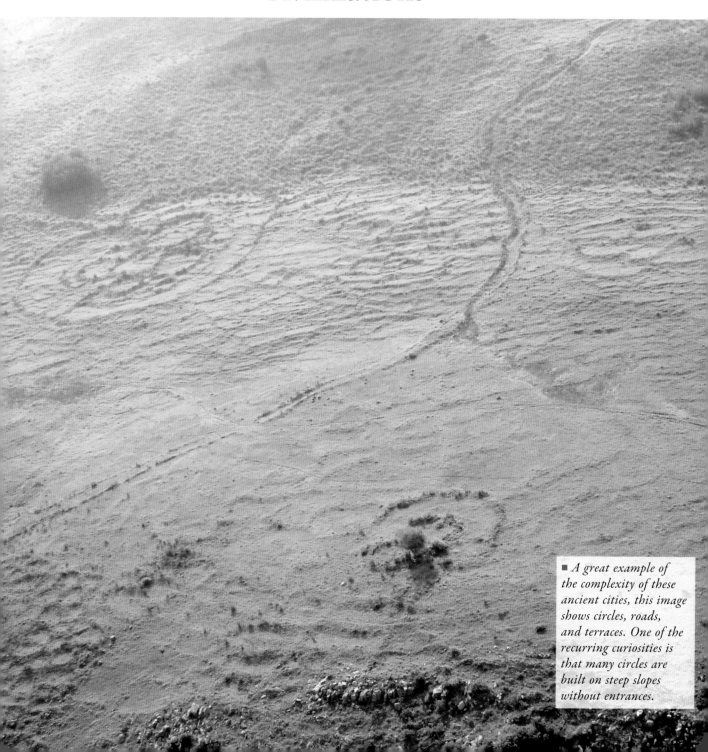

■ *A great example of the complexity of these ancient cities, this image shows circles, roads, and terraces. One of the recurring curiosities is that many circles are built on steep slopes without entrances.*

■ *When you explore these ruins there is no suggestion at all that you are walking over extended sections of the circles. It is only from the air that you realize how the circles were all linked by a never-ending web of stone structures. So when you look at these aerial photos, look at the spaces between the circles. Therein lies the real mystery of this vanished civilization.*

UNTIL RECENTLY, IT was estimated that there are around 20,000 mysterious stone ruins scattered throughout southern Africa. This was a conclusion reached by the Zimbabwean archaeologist Roger Summers in the early 1970s. Summers researched these structures extensively—especially Great Zimbabwe—and studied the work of earlier explorers like Theodore Bent, R. N. Hall, W. G. Neal, and others. In 1891 Theodore Bent estimated that about 4,000 ruins were scattered in this part of the world. My own research of the past several years, which includes thousands of aerial photographs and hiking through hundreds of kilometers of mountainous terrain, physically exploring thousands of these stone structures, has shown that there are well over 100,000 of these mysterious stone ruins.

In a telephone conversation I had with Professor Revil Mason, retired head of archaeology at the University of the Witwatersrand, in September 2008, he concurred with my estimate of about 100,000 of these stone structure in South Africa. This instantly presented a problem regarding the population that would have been required to erect such a large number of structures. When I suggested that it would have taken a population of at least one million people in southern Africa at some historic point in time, he quickly dismissed such theories and concluded that there could not be 100,000 ruins. After all, all our history books clearly tell us that this was a sparsely populated part of the world—certainly there were not millions of people milling around. This is just another perfect example of reverse logic and unintelligible reasoning from intelligent people.

The mystery deepens when we look at the extent and complexity of these ruins. These stone settlements are not merely scattered, isolated structures or small clusters of stone remains but rather large, densely populated settlements and communities linked by extensive agricultural terraces and connected by ancient roads that seem to stretch from Mozambique to Botswana and probably beyond. The extended ancient settlement that connects Waterval Boven, Machadodorp, and Carolina covers an area much larger than Johannesburg today. While many have been destroyed by forestry, farming, and roadwork, there are still breathtaking examples of these ruins with walls wider than 2 meters and 3 meters high. The entire area of ruins and terraces includes all the countries of southern Africa and covers more than 500,000 square kilometers.

The latest scrutiny of the land using satellite technology reveals even more unbelievable results. No one could have been prepared for the staggering numbers of ruined structures I have discovered: at least one million. This number is so large that it completely and utterly shatters any other previous ideas I had held about these mysterious and vanished civilizations, our ancient past, and the magnificent lost cities of southern Africa. In the next chapter, "Calculating the Impossible," I will discuss these calculations in more detail.

The following image goes a long way toward supporting the research of Ann Kritzinger from Zimbabwe University showing these were not dwellings, animal pits, or storage silos but rather work stations and leaching tanks for the processing and extraction of gold or other metals. The strange honeycomb structure also suggests that sound energy was used in erecting these structures so that they could harness the energy directly from the Earth—as demonstrated by Tesla in the late nineteenth century.

In nature many structures take on a hexagonal shape because of its strength and fundamental link to the flow of energy (see the chapter titled "Measurements" about the Hexagon ruin, page 73). These ruins are clustered together just like a natural honeycomb. Did this encourage the flow of specific vibrational energy to help extract the gold? This kind of technique is not new to industry. Vibrational frequencies are used in many applications to separate substances.

Moreover, as the image on page 88 shows, the large patterns along which these settlements were structured vividly resemble sound vibration patterns. The builders must have had the knowledge to identify the vibrational energy fields in the ground and then built the walls along those lines. This is the most scientific explanation for these patterns. Note that there is always a road (connector) linking the circles into the external matrix.

■ *Many small circles, clustered together like a honeycomb, are still visible from the air.*

■ *Close-up of a honeycomb*

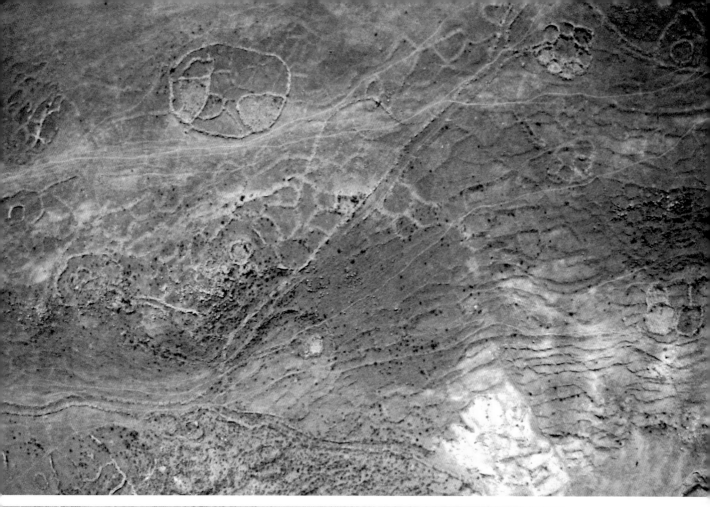

■ *When the grass has burned in winter, the full extent of the vanished cities becomes evident. There were dwellings and terraces, work stations, and places of worship and ceremony. The ancient city covered an area much larger than modern-day Los Angeles.*

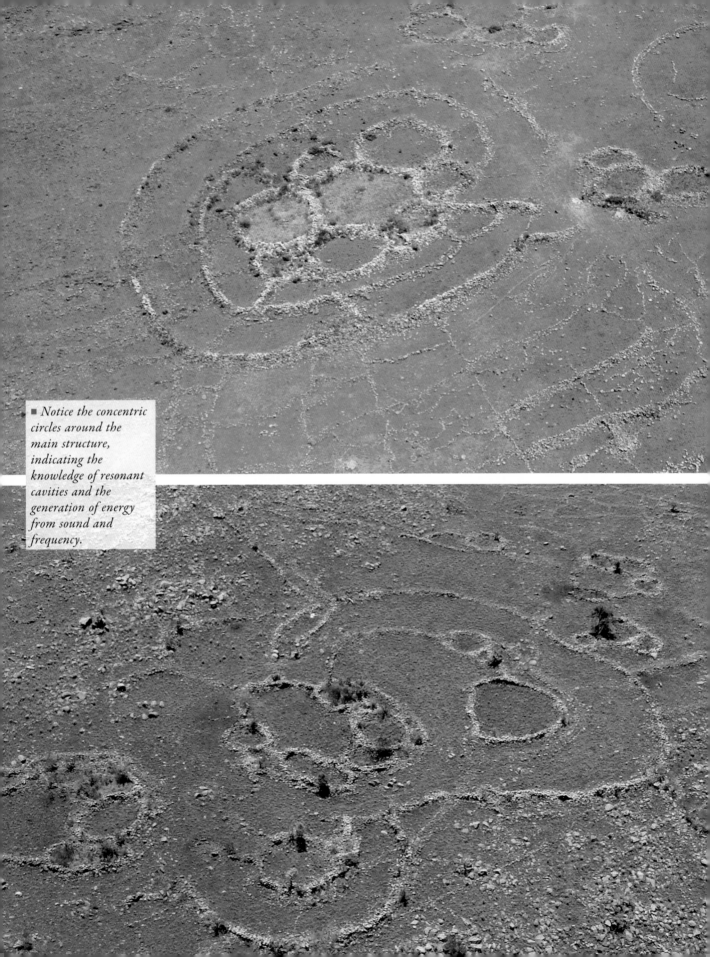

■ *Notice the concentric circles around the main structure, indicating the knowledge of resonant cavities and the generation of energy from sound and frequency.*

■ *Once again—look at the spaces between the obvious circles.*

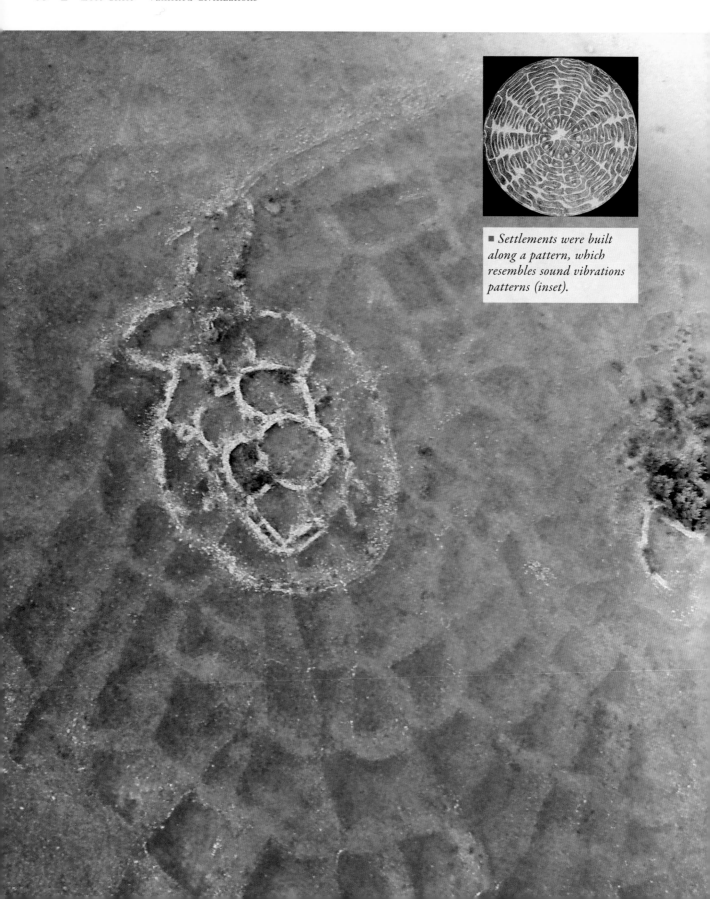

■ *Settlements were built along a pattern, which resembles sound vibrations patterns (inset).*

■ *Multiple circles with*
channels connecting them

Calculating
the Impossible

I MAPPED CONTINUOUS settlements that cover thousands of square kilometers between South Africa, Botswana, and Zimbabwe. I calculated the average number of circular structures per hectare, per square kilometer, and the full extent of these settlements. My immediate estimate was that there would be at least one million ruined stone structures. Obviously my immediate response was what everyone would have thought: "That is impossible." However, the calculations are even more staggering.

There are at least three densely populated areas or lost cities, each one stretching for about 100 kilometers by 100 kilometers, covering about 10,000 square kilometers. To put this into perspective, each one of these areas is larger than modern-day Johannesburg (or Los Angeles, for those who are less familiar with South Africa). I found an average 3.62 ruins per hectare. This adds up to 362 ruins per square kilometer, which eventually gives us the previously unimaginable number of 3.62 million stone ruins per one ancient city. The total number of ruins in all three lost cities adds up to 10.86 million circular stone ruins. I need to remind you that there are more "lost cities" out there, I have just not had the time to evaluate all of them yet.

■ *All the circles were connected by the strange walled channels. Though I use the term* road *for simplicity's sake, we must recognize that clearly they were something else—something more fundamental to the construction of the ancient cities. The only theory that holds any merit so far is that they were energy channels—using the natural conductive material in the stone to do so. Remember that this stone is at least 50 percent silica or quartzite—the building blocks of quartz crystals. And silica is a great conductor of not only light and information, as in fiber optics and silicon chips, but also sound energy.*

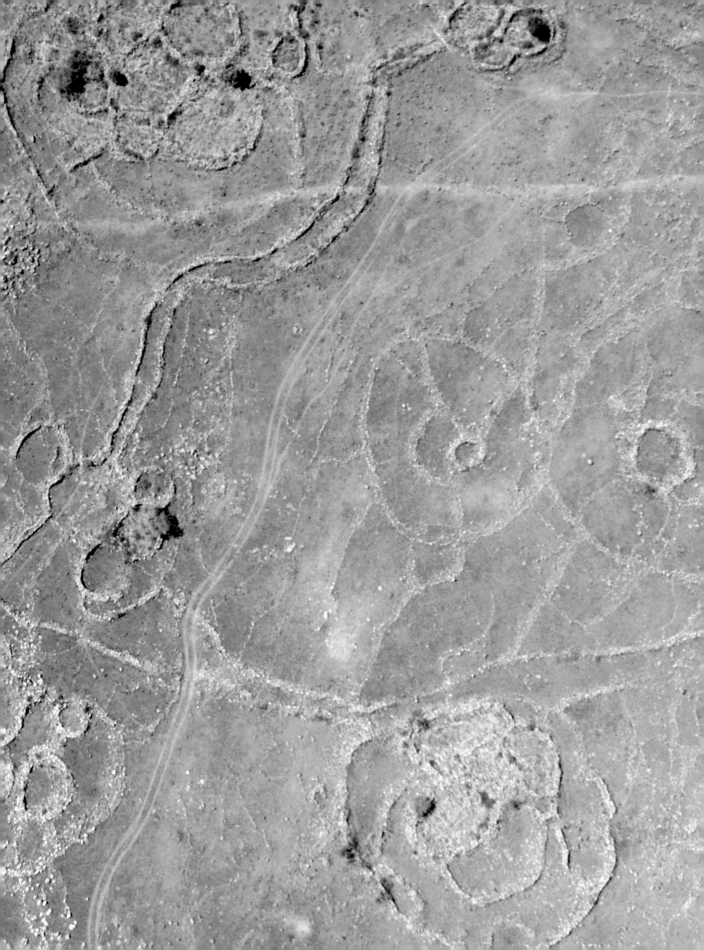

■ *These first satellite images (above and on facing page) show a close-up view of the density of the lost cities. Even these images show the covered structures under the soil that once connected all of the stone circles.*

Further calculations reveal the following:*

Average number of stones per square meter	30
Stones per depth of wall	5
Avg. number of stones per running meter of wall—1 m high	150
Number of stones per 2 m high wall	300
Average length of wall in avg. stone circle	30
Total number of stones in average circle	9,000
Average weight per stone in kilograms	20
Average weight of stone in one circle—metric tons	180
Total number of stones in one lost city	(32.58 billion) 32,580,000,000
Total weight of stones in kilograms in one lost city	(651 billion) 651,600,000,000

This new information forces us to reevaluate what we thought we knew about the mysterious civilizations of southern Africa and its inhabitants who built these ancient cities.

---

*For the purpose of my calculation I estimated that the original wall height was 2 meters—a very conservative estimate considering it is still 3 meters high in some well-preserved examples.

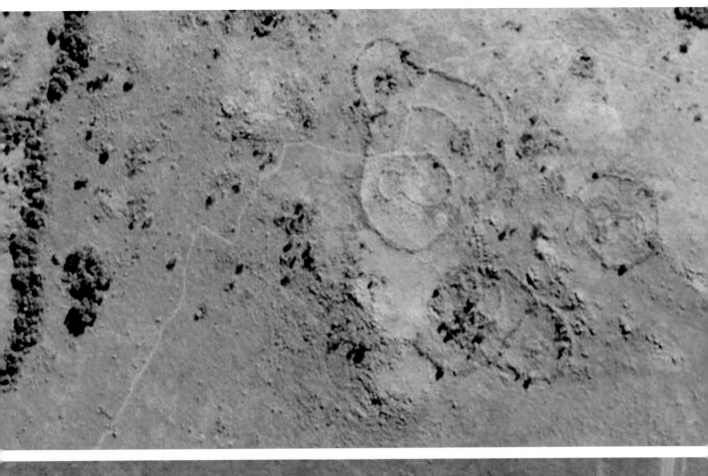

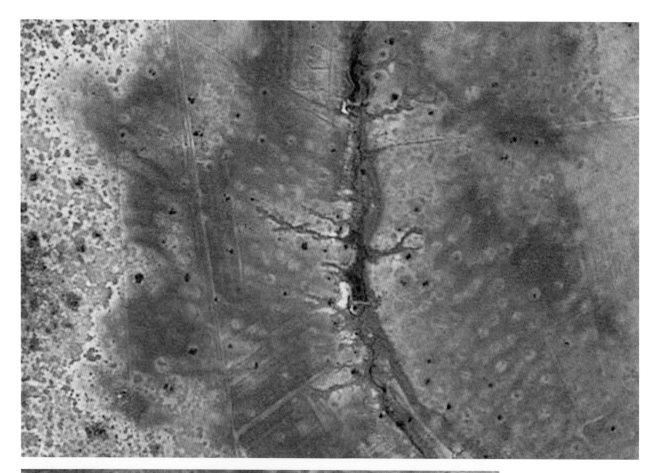

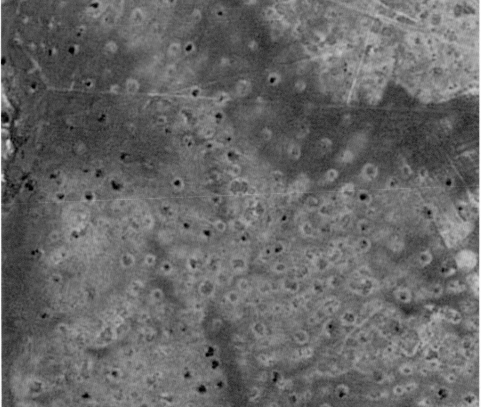

■ *A view from a much higher elevation shows that the circles can even be seen under the soil in plowed fields, where crops have been farmed for decades.*

■ *(right) In the African bush, trees grow in clusters and in circular patterns around the wall remains. This becomes visible after becoming acclimatized to observing these patterns from satellite images over some time.*

The Oldest
Agricultural Terraces

■ *Two roads join
halfway up a
mountain in the
middle of an extended
agricultural terrace.
Some circles can be
seen among all of this.*

IT WAS REPORTED by Summers in the 1970s—and others before him—that the ancient agricultural terraces in Zimbabwe (formerly called Rhodesia) cover about 190,000 square kilometers. This may at first sound a little outrageous, but when you start to explore the ruins across the border in South Africa, you realize that the ancient terraces continue indefinitely in this part of the world, covering many more thousands of square kilometers. These defy previous understanding about the ancient population numbers in southern Africa. My latest research suggests that there was an ancient civilization of many millions of people who constructed millions of stone circles and needed all these terraces to survive.

The meticulous construction of these terraces, all lined with rock walls, is staggering. Billions of large and small stones were used to construct terraces of different sizes. Many are built on very steep mountain slopes, and the height of some terraces exceeds 3 to 5 meters. Some of the terraces are strategically placed around a water source on the mountain. Some of the gullies show scattered rock in a concentrated area around the stream, which could be the possible remains of a dam. The stored water would have been used for agriculture, and also possibly for other purposes. Many of the terraces are sloped in such a way that would allow the water to move slowly with gravity, gradually from one level to the next. There is not only one kind of terrace. I have clearly identified terraces that were used for grazing domesticated animals and other terraces for cultivating crops. Many of the so-called roads or channels run straight down the mountains, ending in small rivers and streams. This remains a highly curious aspect of the channels.

HOW OLD ARE THESE TERRACES?

In his book *Time Detectives,* Brian Fagan describes how botanist-archaeologists, or archaeobotanists, excavated similar agricultural terraces in Peru and Egypt to analyze the ancient crops of the lands. Their discoveries were staggering: the earliest crops in Egypt were planted as far back as 18,000 years ago, and South America was not far behind. Sadly, such research on the ancient terraces in South Africa has not been performed, but initial archaeological analysis of some of these ancient terraces indicates that they could be older than 5,000 years. Once again, we need to remind ourselves that if this is in fact the Cradle of Humankind, and if this is where the first humans developed and began to grasp the concepts of art and survival, is it not possible that they could have grasped the art of cultivation long before the rest of the world? The sheer size of the lost civilization and dates ascribed to it suggest that these are in fact the

■ *This large rock near the top of a mountain at Waterval Boven was once the conduit for a spring water source situated behind it and stretching all the way down to the Elands River. The rock is on the edge of a settlement of circles, which are now covered by trees. This was all destroyed, along with countless other ruins, by the roadwork when the N4 highway was built. We trust that the Roads Agency will become aware of this and start behaving responsibly toward preserving those ruins that have not been completely destroyed along the highways.*

oldest and the first agricultural terraces on Earth—but much more scientific work needs to be done.

In 2003 archaeologists with the Amapa Institute of Scientific and Technological Research uncovered the impressive ruins of an ancient stone monolith observatory site at Macapa, near Brazil's border with French Guyana. This came as quite a shock to archaeologists as they did not expect such activity by ancient tribes in that part of the world. Archaeologist Mariana Petry Cabral of the Amapa Institute said that "only a society with a complex culture could have built such a monument." These ruins are estimated to be 2,000 years old at a guess, but are probably much older. Large settlements that cover more than 1,000 square kilometers, surrounded by terraces and roads—similar to the ones in South Africa—have been discovered deeper in the jungles of Brazil. It seems that there were ancient civilizations all over the world that are now causing archaeologists and historians to reconsider the activities of ancient man on planet Earth. Africa, however, remains the first.

■ *A spectacular view of ancient terraces and the complexity of their structure—against a steep slope toward the river.*

■ *Once your eye gets tuned in, and you recognize the signs, you will see ancient terraces everywhere.*

■ *This is what covered terraces look like under the trees. To most it will just be a strange outcrop of stones along the slope, but thousands of terraces just like this one lie hidden below the overgrowth of trees.*

■ *Stones from structures and terraces roll down the mountain. To the untrained eye it simply looks like natural stones rolling down from the mountaintop.*

Ancient Roads
and Mysterious Energy

UNTIL YOU STUDY the ruins from the air it is impossible to get a realistic idea of the size and scale of the settlements. While the walls that still stand above the ground attract our attention immediately, there seems to be a never-ending grid of walls that link them all together like a giant spider's web. This

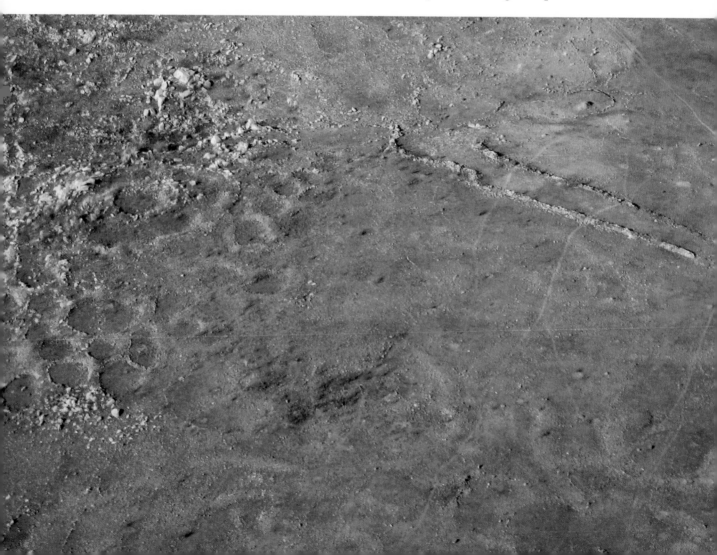

large and extended web of walls is covered by the sand and cannot be seen or detected while walking among the ruins—this is an important bit of information to digest. We have found no record of any excavations or detailed research into this extended web of covered settlements.

It is also only from the air that you can identify the continuous ancient roads that link all these stone settlements. We have identified at least 500 kilometers of them. If these roads serviced this ancient civilization effectively, they must have originally run all the way from the Mozambican coast to a number of destinations inland as far as Botswana and Zimbabwe—an area of thousands of kilometers. More aerial exploration will most likely expose the hidden roads that currently appear and disappear along the way.

For now we have traced the ancient roads from Barberton through Waterval Boven, to Carolina, Belfast, Middelburg, Bronkhorstspruit, and past Rustenburg to Swartruggens into Botswana. The road system spreads out to the north, through Pietersburg into Zimbabwe. The well-preserved examples of the roads are always lined by stone walls on both sides of the road. In some places

■ *A stunning view of a connecting channel running through what was a dense settlement, now completely destroyed and covered by soil. It runs up a slope where it ends in the very distinct honeycomb remains of a very densely arranged structure. I believe that these were ancient leaching tanks for the processing and extraction of metals—most probably gold. (Photo by Gustav van Rensburg.)*

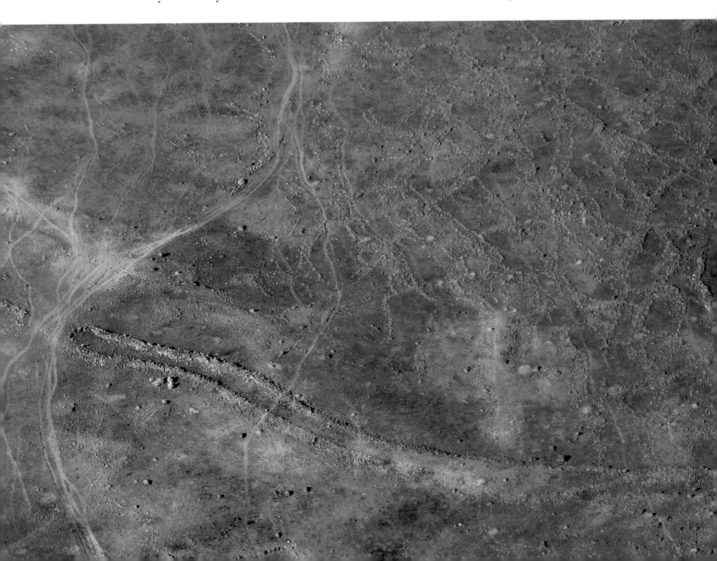

these stone edges are more than 1.5 meters high, as you can see in the above image. This remains the greatest mystery of the ancient roads. Why would anyone need to border all their roads and paths with walls consisting of millions of stones?

Based on our scrutiny of these ancient roads, we calculated that it required more than 500 million large stones to build only the sections of the road that we have identified. This is an engineering feat of some magnitude and cannot be ascribed to migrating tribes from the north who built paths for their cattle . . . as is often described by some academics. There is no civilization in history who built all their roads lined by walls. There is no documented record in history that outlines such a large-scale construction of roads by the people in southern Africa. This raises many questions about identity of the builders of these ancient roads, when the roads were built, and for what purpose. Not to mention, what mode of transport did they use if the wheel only arrived in southern Africa with the Portuguese explorers in the late 1400s?

These roads appear and disappear in places and weave their way between the stone ruins and settlements. In some sections they run up very steep hills, indicating that the road users had a very advanced way of transporting goods—it is not possible for horses or cattle to pull loaded wagons up such steep inclines. Therefore we have to contemplate a whole new theory for these channels and their use.

As laughable as it may sound to some, one technology used on these ancient channels could have been a levitation vehicle that somehow tapped in to the magnetic content of the stones along the sides. The iron levels in the stones are

■ *Toward the right edge of this image is a good example of how recent inhabitants used the stones to erect a more angular structure for their own needs. It is quite common that in the stone circle ruins we find square structures, which were adapted by later civilization.*

■ *A short section of an ancient connecting channel runs up a steep hill, right past more stone circles overgrown by trees. This channel was also destroyed by roadwork.*

very high and have conductive and magnetic properties; these are crucial facts for investigation. This levitation theory could be why the roads have continuous walls marking the edges, similar to how modern trains float above their electromagnetic tracks without any friction. Look at the many photos that clearly show channels connecting to stone circles and then connecting to other circles like a network of railway tracks.

■ *Energy channels
connecting stone circles*

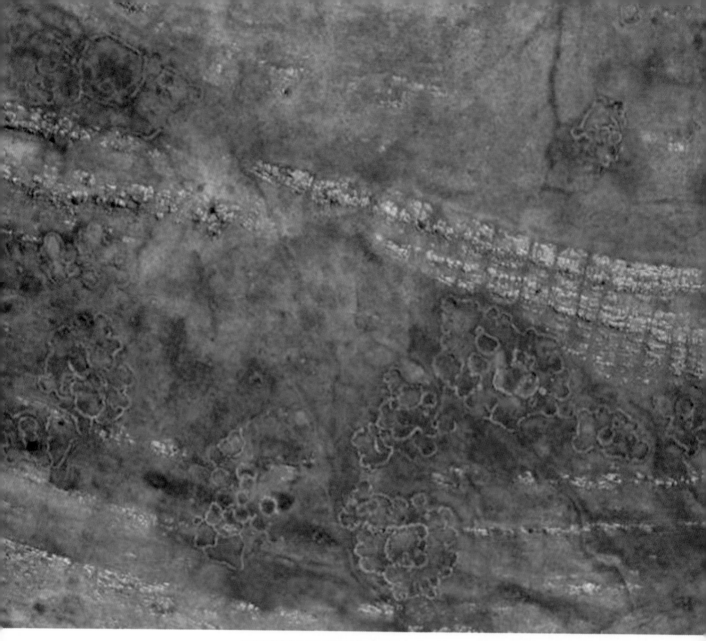

■ *These satellite pictures show the remains of intricate ruins at Bronkhorstspruit, South Africa. The short connecting channels link the ruins to the main channel bottom right of the picture. The spaces between the ruins are not empty but more ruins covered by soil.*

■ *The author indicates the channel linking into a stone circle ruin. The channels often run into the center of the circle, where they end with no exit possible, and no doors.*

■ *A well-preserved channel runs along a mountaintop, with many stone circles that once linked to it with shorter channels.*

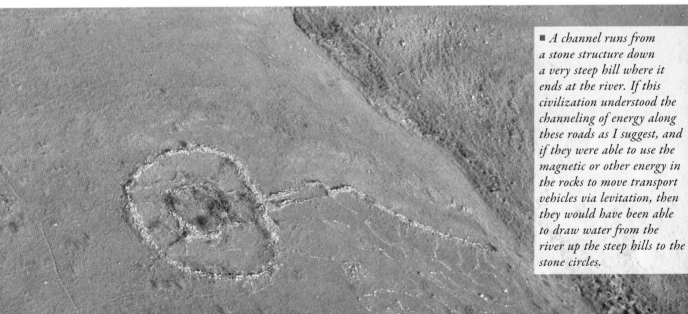

■ *A channel runs from a stone structure down a very steep hill where it ends at the river. If this civilization understood the channeling of energy along these roads as I suggest, and if they were able to use the magnetic or other energy in the rocks to move transport vehicles via levitation, then they would have been able to draw water from the river up the steep hills to the stone circles.*

■ *Another channel runs up a steep hill where it abruptly ends. It suggests that there was a stone circle which has since been completely destroyed.*

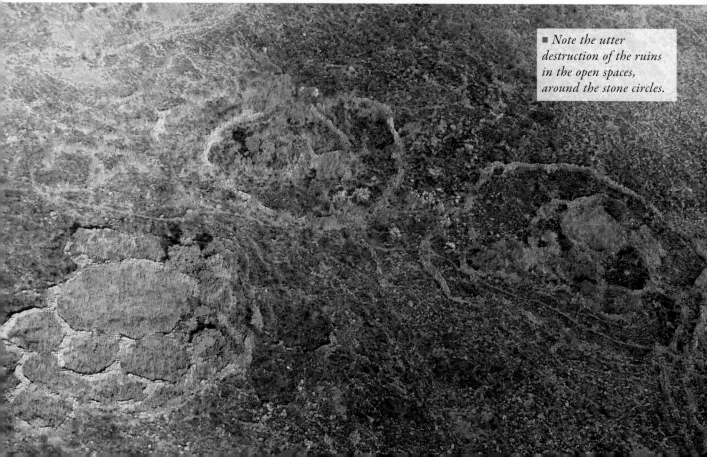

■ *Note the utter destruction of the ruins in the open spaces, around the stone circles.*

■ *The channel can still clearly be seen, but the circle it once ran in to is almost completely destroyed.*

Ancient Levitation Device and White Powder of Gold

BEFORE YOU CALL me crazy, let me quickly remind you of the most famous levitation device on Earth, and the most sought-after artifact in history: the biblical ark of the covenant. We are constantly reminded in the Bible that the ark never touched the ground and that it always hovered several inches above the earth. From its construction of gold we can calculate that the ark weighed between three and four tons. We are also told that it was carried by four men. This could obviously not be possible; therefore, the four men must have pushed the levitating ark as they walked.

Over the years there have been many speculations about the real contents of the ark, besides the fabled tablets of the Ten Commandments. Some researchers have suggested that manna from heaven was a white powdery substance, which Moses fed to the Israelites in the morning mixed with a little bit of dew. This white powdery substance has been identified by several scholars, such as Sir Laurence Gardner and David Hudson, as "white powder of gold" or the "mono-atomic" form of gold. It is also called the Philosopher's Stone, the Elixir of Life, and Star Fire in mystic circles and by alchemists of the past.

Leading science laboratories have done research into this phenomenon and presented astonishing new information that shatters all our pervious perceptions regarding life itself. Hudson calls this mono-atomic form of gold "ORMEs"— Orbitally Rearranged Mono-atomic Elements. The study of the chemistry and physics of mono-atomic elements describes the characteristics of those elements that we know as the precious metals. These eight metals include ruthenium, rhodium, palladium, and silver (known as the "light platinum group"); osmium, iridium, platinum, and gold (known as the "heavy platinum group").

Just before you wonder what all this has to do with ancient ruins and the Bible and Moses and the ark, let me remind you what Moses did when he came down from the mountain with the Ten Commandments: he took the golden calf and burned it in the fire. He then transformed the golden calf *not* into molten liquid gold, but into white powder. Then he took this powder, dissolved it in water, and made the Israelites drink the water (Exodus 32:20). Does this make any sense at all? Of course not—not until we discover the true properties of this white powder of gold, and then suddenly this mysterious part of our history books and the Bible makes a lot more sense.

The white, fluffy, powdery substance has the following properties: When exposed to a very small electrical charge it absorbs the energy and stores it. It behaves like a capacitor and energy storage device—not a conductor as some may think. It does, however, behave as a superconductor, conducting information instantly between one end and the other. The powder also responds to tiny amounts of energy in a way that, when it is exposed to minute amounts of energy, it floats and defies the laws of gravity. Hudson reports that in the lab, when he brought his hand up below the flask, the low levels of energy in his hand caused the powder inside the flask to lift up and float. It had no such reaction, however, to magnets or any other material tested. This suggests that there are traces of mono-atomic elements in our bodies, which repel the powder—just like the positive poles on two magnets repel each other. But the best part of Hudson's research is that at between 700–800°C the powder disappears completely from sight. It leaves this dimension and enters another. As the

■ *Depiction of the ark of the covenant*

temperature is reduced, the powder miraculously reappears at the same temperature at which it disappeared. According to Hudson, this is the information that the Massachusetts Institute of Technology (MIT) has been very secretive about and refused to publish any papers on.

Furthermore, the energized powder is reported to give off a bright white light previously not seen by humans. This is a single-frequency white light and not the light that breaks up into the primary colors of the rainbow. If you think this is all too much . . . wait . . . there is more. The healing properties of the powder are most mysterious and this is most likely what Moses was doing in the desert. He was healing his people. In one of his recorded video lectures, Gardner reported on experiments performed by European scientists to determine the effect of white powder of gold on human DNA strands. The presence of the white light seems to repair all genetic defects in our DNA, and it heals human cells from any disease they may exhibit. This is most likely what Royal Raymond Rife discovered in 1931, when he reportedly found the "cure for all disease." A banquet was held in his honor on November 20, 1931, in Pasadena, California, where forty-four of the leading medical experts announced "the end to all disease." Sadly, this discovery was very quickly covered up by the pharmaceutical fraternity when they realized that this was a real discovery and would undoubtedly cause their demise. Rife is reported to have used a range of vibrational frequencies of sound and a specific frequency of "white light" to cure cancerous cells at will in his laboratory.

With this bit of information it suddenly makes a whole lot of sense why Moses would have given this powder to his people. They could not have been a clean bunch, without water and sanitation in the desert for forty years. They must have been full of disease, and their minds were probably not very clear either. This white powder of gold has been a very well-guarded secret for thousands of years among alchemists and healers. Because the first gold mines on Earth were located in southern Africa, it would make sense that the early authorities—namely the Anunnaki under the leadership of Enki—would have used the advanced properties of gold to make life a little easier. It also explains how the ancients could have moved the ten-ton stones used in their construction of Adam's Calendar and other megalithic sites with relative ease.

The ark would hiss and buzz and spark and shoot out long flames. No one but the chosen few were allowed near it, and it had to be covered by a special cloak to contain its fury. It killed Aaron's two sons when they disobeyed a command and lifted the veil to have a closer look. For those who still find this a little far-fetched, let me remind you that the ark was also used for a number of practical purposes by Joshua. He defeated several armies many times the size of his own army by simply placing the ark in their way; it brought down the walls of Jericho by using the energy inside as a resonant harmonic vibration to destabilize the walls; it parted the waters of the river Jordan; and it also parted the waters of the Red Sea. This may come as a surprise to some, in which case I suggest you read your Bible properly—especially the book of Joshua, where it is made very clear that Moses was already in possession of the ark when leaving Egypt. All of this was possible because the ark contained the most precious and mysterious substance in all of human history: white powder of gold.

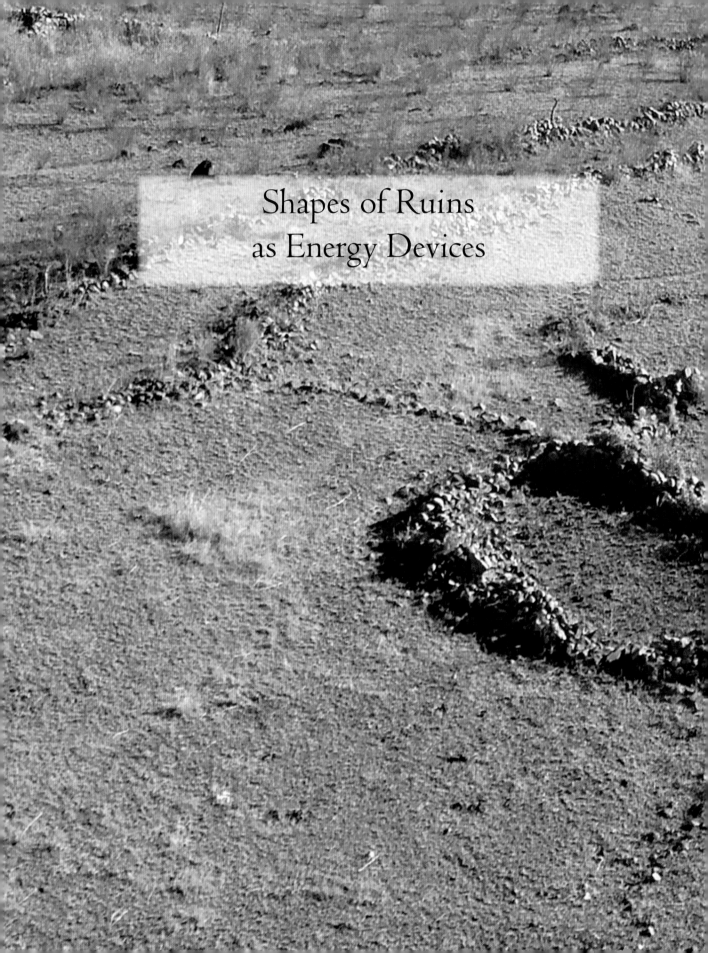

Shapes of Ruins
as Energy Devices

■ *Could these circles have generated energy in ancient times?*

THE UNIVERSAL CIRCULAR structure of these ruins suggests that this shape was intentional on the part of the builders and furnished some sort of benefit. At first we are told that this is the simplest way to construct a building, but the truth may be a little bit more involved. The way that most of the stone circles in southern Africa are connected by paths and roads is very puzzling. From the air it looks just like a modern city with roads leading up to every driveway, with the glaring difference being the ancient roads are lined with stone walls, still standing 1.5 meters high in places. It makes no sense why every ancient ruin would have required the road to run right into it.

One of the great puzzles of the stone circles is the absence of doors or entrances in many of the ruins. And where there are entrances they seem to have been constructed by later inhabitants with different needs. In many places, at the point where the road meets the stone circle, there is a stone wall that meets the road. In some ruins the road leads into the center of the circular structure and dead-ends. This "end" of the road is surrounded by a number of smaller circles, all of which are inside the large outside wall. Images of these constructions are on the following pages.

We simply cannot continue our conventional way of thinking about these structures, and we will have to think out-of-the-box to solve this mystery. There is simply no explanation why a large circular stone structure with a diameter of 25 to 150 meters, which contains a number of smaller circular stone structures, would be constructed without any entrances. It gets even more weird: many of the internal stone circles also have no entrances and simply look like a cluster of grapes inside an outer wall.

Our first reaction to the ancient roads was obvious, because we think in terms of what we know and experience today. Our first reaction was that they *must* be roads, because they remind us of roads and they seem to link all these ruins together.

As mentioned in preceding chapters, I have come to the conclusion that they are not roads as we think of them, but energy channels—connection devices. Those who know a little bit about electronics and the generation of energy will instantly see the similarity between many of the ruins' shapes and modern devices used in laser technology and other advanced applications. The magnetron—which is used for generating vibrational frequency energy in many modern appliances like microwaves—is virtually a copy of many of the flower-shaped stone structures. The magnetron's relative, the klystron, also has myriad applications, such as radar. The following image, with the inset of a magnetron, highlights this incredible resemblance.

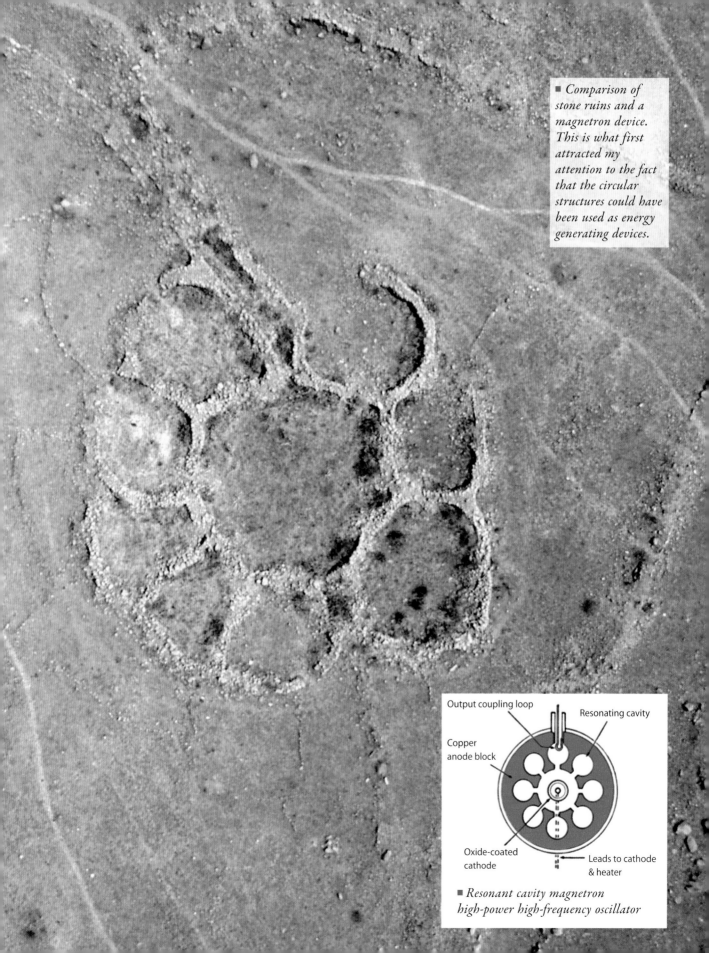

■ *Comparison of stone ruins and a magnetron device. This is what first attracted my attention to the fact that the circular structures could have been used as energy generating devices.*

Output coupling loop

Resonating cavity

Copper anode block

Oxide-coated cathode

Leads to cathode & heater

■ *Resonant cavity magnetron high-power high-frequency oscillator*

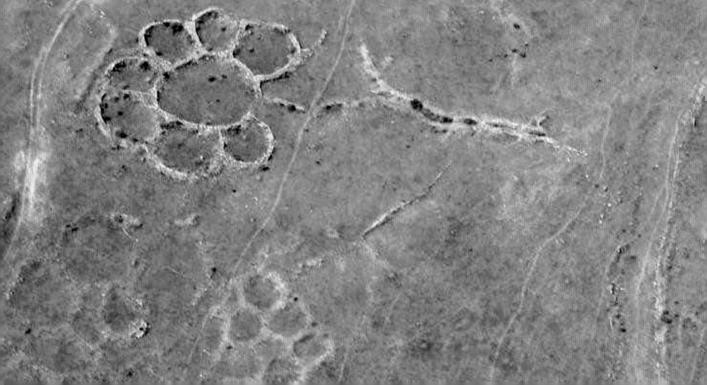

The energy connections do not end there: some ruins still have the central monolith that can be compared to the central high-frequency oscillator in the magnetron energy device. This central rod, or stone, is made to vibrate at a specific frequency that is amplified in the adjacent resonant chambers and then channeled out via the connectors that conduct the vibrational energy to another destination, where it is used in many possible ways. The original vibration in the center of the magnetron, or circle, can be generated by sound. The frequency or pitch of the sound will create the specific energy required to perform various tasks. These tasks can vary from magnetism to drilling to levitation, and many more. Sound impossible? It's not. John Worrell Keely did something quite similar in 1888.

Isn't it strange how we seem to rediscover ancient knowledge as we move into the future? Most, if not all, devices used to generate energy in modern times are circular or spherical. I suggest that this was also the case in ancient times before we lost such knowledge—along with everything else that we rediscovered in the past century. The many patent drawings of Nikola Tesla outlining the generation and distribution of free energy are also very similar in their circular structure to the stone circles of southern Africa. Stone circles are not unique to southern Africa. They have been found all over the world, in the most distant and unimaginable places—often in dense formations similar to those in southern Africa. Examples include the desert plain of northern Chile, in the United States in the ocean off the coast of Florida, as well as in Jordan where there are thousands of circles that also seem to show the remains of channels that once connected them.

In his excellent book *The Gods' Machines,* which covers hundreds of ancient sites and structures from all over the world, researcher Wun Chok Bong shows in great detail how all these ancient structures were used as energy devices in some way or another. From Stonehenge to Avebury, these structures were not a simple assembly of stones to mark the rise of the sun on some arbitrary day. Bong did not include any of the stone ruins of southern Africa in his research. This is mainly because these stones represent the most mysterious of all the lost civilizations on Earth, and second because until recently they were referred to as cattle kraals. The energy creating principle is the only scientifically sound theory so far, and it is instantly applicable to the stone ruins of southern Africa.

■ *The channels connect directly into the center of the stone circles and connect with one of the circular resonating cavities, making it very clear that the architects of these structures knew exactly what they were doing. They probably used the vibrational frequency of sound to generate energy, magnified it in the circular resonating chambers, and then channeled it down the two stone-wall connectors to feed into the larger energy grid of the entire settlement.*

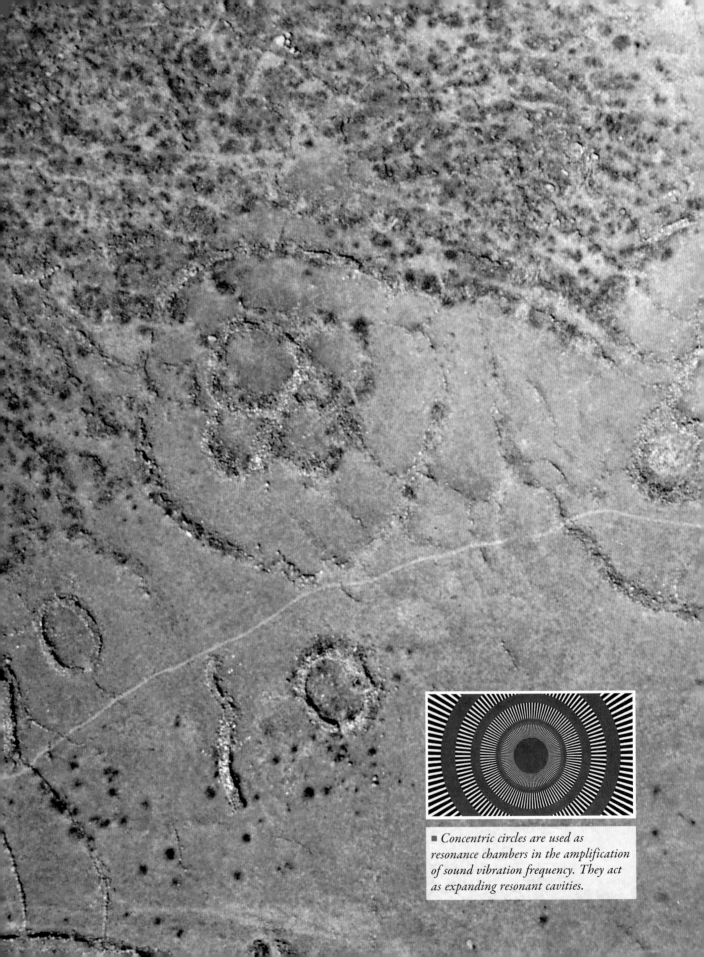

■ *Concentric circles are used as resonance chambers in the amplification of sound vibration frequency. They act as expanding resonant cavities.*

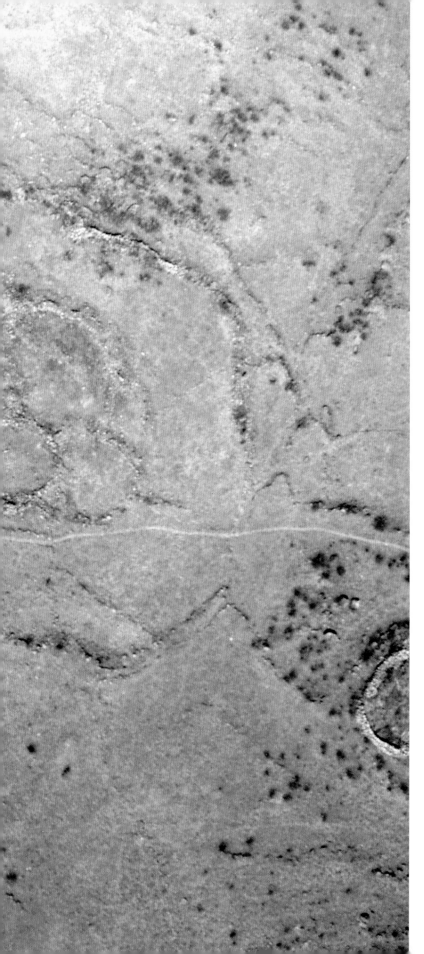

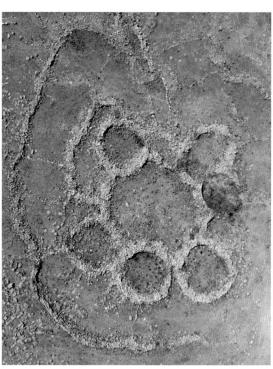

■ *Just one of many spectacular examples of circular stone structures with external resonant chambers and walls to create and amplify energy to be used in all kinds of ways.*

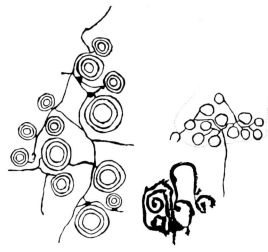

■ *These are archaeological sketches of stone ruins near the Nooitgedacht Dam. They resemble resonant chambers for the generation of energy. Some are more advanced, showing three concentric walls for greater resonance and amplification. The roads can be seen as the wires that link them all together and channel the energy into the greater settlement grid.*

Population Mystery

THE LARGE CONTINUOUS distribution of stone settlements and terraces and ancient roads in southern Africa—which cover several hundred thousand square kilometers—raises a very important question: How many people must have lived here to need such a large, expansive network of settlements?

When we examine the southern African population models of the past 1,000 years, it simply makes no sense. The estimated number of black South Africans during the time of the South African War in 1900 was 800,000 people. The total estimated population of South Africa was no more than 1 million. The estimated population of the Basotho people during the time of establishing the kingdom of Lesotho in the early 1800s was around 20,000 people.

The current theory is that migrating tribes from northeast Africa would have moved in small individual groups of a few dozen at a time. The largest group would have been no more than around 300 people. These settlers would almost have behaved like hunter-gatherers, even though they built permanent settlements. They adopted a nomadic lifestyle, always ready to pack up and move in a short space of time because of wild animals, weather, or other warring tribes. They certainly did not have the kind of labor force and lifestyle to build millions of stone circles consisting of billions of heavy rocks, complex stone calendars, and roads that stretch for hundreds of kilometers.

Between the years 1900 and 2000 the South African population grew from 1 million to 45 million. This is a growth factor of 45, in 100 years. This means that in 1900 the population was only 2.22% of the population in 2000. Since accurate population statistics do not exist, let us use a simple extrapolation to arrive at some realistic numbers. For the sake of argument, let's be very generous and allow the population to decline by less than a factor of 45. Let's assume that the population shrinks by 70% every 100 years. The following table shows the results of this population model of South Africa for the past 1,000 years.

YEAR AD	POPULATION
2000	45,000,000
1900	1,000,000
1800	300,000
1700	90,000
1600	27,000
1500	8,100
1400	2,430
1300	729

YEAR AD	POPULATION
1200	219
1100	66
1000	20

It is obvious that there is something wrong with this picture. There must have been a time when the population was stable without growth for a long period of time. The survival rate of the inhabitants was low, but somehow they must have kept going without becoming extinct. What this simple exercise does achieve is to point out that there must have been a stable population of indigenous and original inhabitants here that lasted many dozens of thousands of years. They were responsible for the cave art and rock art, which includes paintings, beads, and petroglyphs. Because none of the stone structures have been ascribed to the San or the Khoi people, they must have been constructed by the new settlers from the north.

It is obvious to any sober, thinking person that the millions of stone structures that lie scattered throughout southern Africa could simply not have been built by those migrating settlers from the north, nor a handful of hunter-gatherers who may have lived here. This forces us to look for new answers and not allow us to be blinded by past perceptions.

Although we sometimes tend to deny it, South Africa is going through a highly politicized phase. While some of us are driven by strong pride in our own culture and unshakable faith in our ancestors, others have a strong tendency to correct the wrongs of the past with sometimes questionable actions. No matter what our individual liberal, political, or historic views may be, the real ancient history of South Africa needs to be thoroughly examined. There were simply not enough people here between the eleventh and eighteenth centuries AD to build all these ruins and the infrastructure that surrounds them.

We should not be surprised that the Sumerians, the first apparent civilization on Earth, give us very clear clues about what was going on in this part of the world thousands of years ago—long before any of us could have imagined.

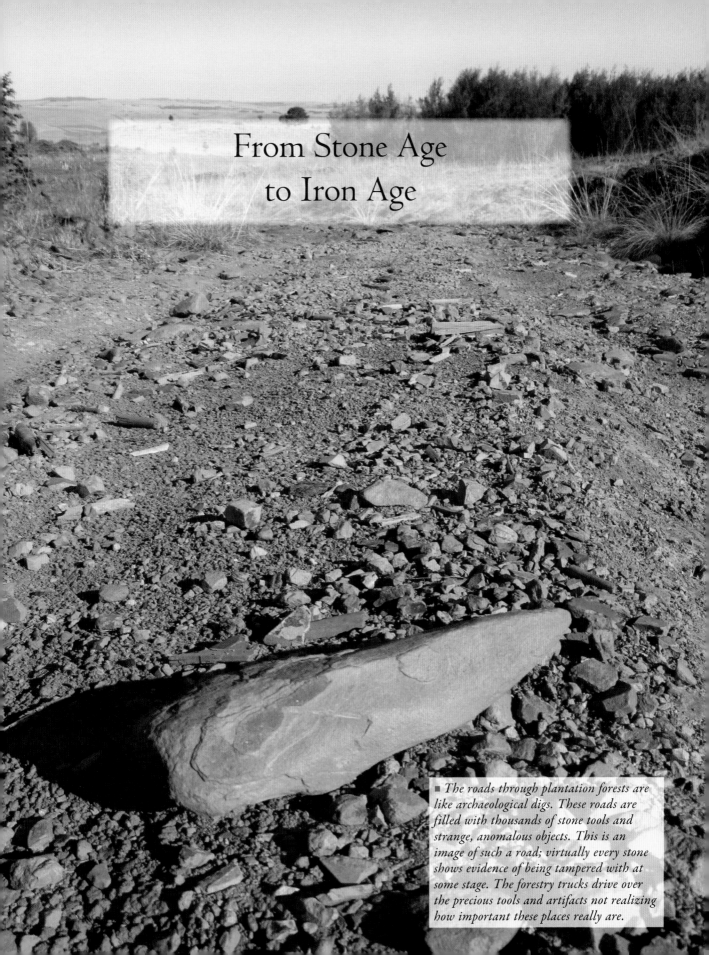

From Stone Age
to Iron Age

■ *The roads through plantation forests are like archaeological digs. These roads are filled with thousands of stone tools and strange, anomalous objects. This is an image of such a road; virtually every stone shows evidence of being tampered with at some stage. The forestry trucks drive over the precious tools and artifacts not realizing how important these places really are.*

SOUTH AFRICA NEVER ceases to provide spectacular evidence of ancient civilizations. In August 2009, University of Cape Town doctorate student Kyle Brown announced a new discovery made at Pinnacle Point in the Western Cape province. This is the abstract to the article, which was published in *Science* magazine:

> The controlled use of fire was a breakthrough adaptation in human evolution. It first provided heat and light and later allowed the physical properties of materials to be manipulated for the production of ceramics and metals. The analysis of tools at multiple sites shows that the source stone materials were systematically manipulated with fire to improve their flaking properties. Heat treatment predominates among silcrete tools at ~72 thousand years ago (ka) and appears as early as 164 ka at Pinnacle Point, on the south coast of South Africa. Heat treatment demands a sophisticated knowledge of fire and an elevated cognitive ability and appears at roughly the same time as widespread evidence for symbolic behavior.

This vital bit of information goes a long way in supporting our discoveries that ancient civilizations flourished in southern Africa in controlled communities—and were much smarter than we had imagined. The large number of anomalous stone tools that we have discovered in the process of exploring the ancient stone ruins is a simple testimony to this. Stone tools that have been shaped with the aid of fire would have been a daily part of the chores and lives of the FIRST people of the south. However, the stone tools and artifacts that I have identified are made of hornfels stone, which splinters and fragments into pieces when exposed to fire. We are therefore not talking about the same events here. The people who built the circles and crafted the anomalous tools certainly did not use fire as a source of heat and energy to make their tools. They had a far more advanced kind of technology and energy that could mold the tools without heating them.

In 1997 a detailed archaeological survey was done of the area surrounding the Nooitgedacht Dam, where sixty-three stone structures were documented and sketched. The team went to a great deal of trouble to catalogue the structures, even recording the GPS points of each one. The report clearly states that based on the number of stone tools discovered in this area, it must have been inhabited for a very long time, stretching over 200,000 years. The most important part of this period would have been the Late Stone Age going back to about 40,000 years, which is most commonly ascribed to the San people, who were also responsible for much of the spectacular rock art in the area.

The researchers then continue to elaborate on the many circular stone structures, which they surveyed with accurate measurements and sketches. Then—for no apparent reason—they claim that these structures were built by people in the Iron Age. They continue their report with a sketch of a single rock carving that depicts what seems to be one of the circular stone structures. For some unknown reason, they report only eighteen engravings in the area.

Johan Heine; Paul van Niekerk, a local farmer; and I recently visited this area with Theunis Niewoudt and his son Ben, another farmer in the area. We photographed more than 100 rock engravings or petroglyphs, which are mostly depictions of the circular stone structures scattered in the veld around them. One of the first things that struck me when looking at the archaeological report was that neither the sketches of the modern-day scholars nor the ancient engravings show any entrances to the stone structures. This applies to the outer walls and the internal circles. And yet, some scholars still continue to insist that these are dwellings.

It is fascinating to note that the report does not mention this crucial information at all. Personally I cannot comprehend how this strange phenomenon has not caused a stampede among archaeologists to decode this mystery. Instead, this question always elicits some ridiculous reply.

People often try to impress others by throwing around words like Iron Age and Stone Age and other potentially confusing archaeological terms. Next time

■ *A few archaeological sketches of so-called Iron Age dwellings. Everyone will immediately notice that these dwellings had no entrances. This is one of the recurring mysteries that some scholars just keep ignoring, and they keep insisting that these were dwellings. The shapes are consistent with our theory of resonant cavities for generating sound energy.*

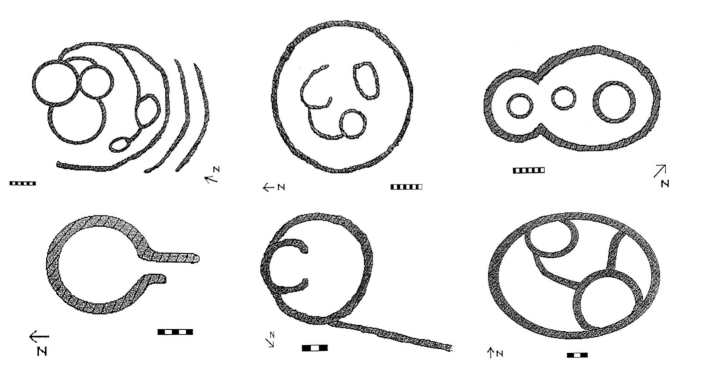

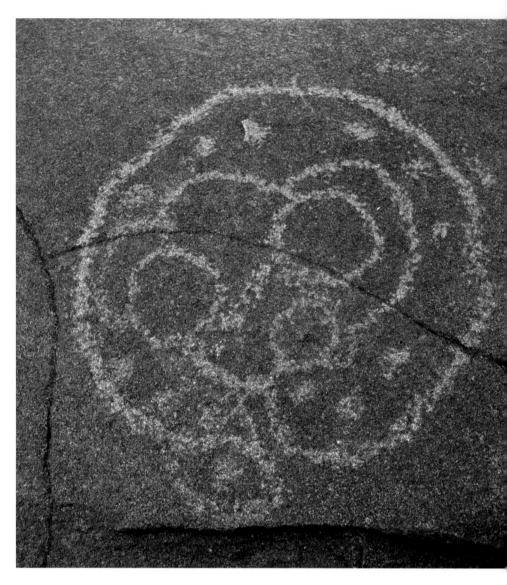

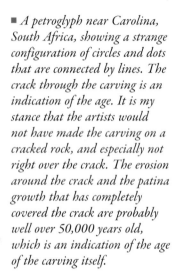

■ *A petroglyph near Carolina, South Africa, showing a strange configuration of circles and dots that are connected by lines. The crack through the carving is an indication of the age. It is my stance that the artists would not have made the carving on a cracked rock, and especially not right over the crack. The erosion around the crack and the patina growth that has completely covered the crack are probably well over 50,000 years old, which is an indication of the age of the carving itself.*

someone mentions Iron Age to you, ask them, "Which Iron Age are you referring to?"

The problem with the Iron Age is that the time line varies dramatically in its appearance from place to place on Earth, starting around 1500 BC in the Near East and Europe; around 1000 BC in the United Kingdom; and receding steadily as we move south to below the Zambezi River, where the current estimated arrival of iron production is between the year 0 and AD 100. The term "early Iron Age" in South Africa is pinned at AD 100–900. Various mysterious tribes like the Lydenburg Culture are linked to this era. In fact the current assumptions of when the various Iron Ages emerged are also guilty of trying to force data to suit the researchers' theories.

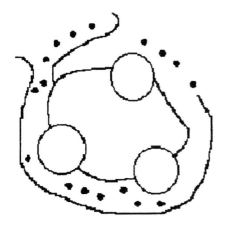

■ *A sketch from 1997 of a similar carving nearby. The little dots on both examples are a real mystery. One theory is that these small piles of stone affected the resonant sound energy generated by the larger circular resonant cavities. They may have changed the frequency of the energy to a lower or higher frequency.*

■ *A set of very sharp and pointed tools found about 10 kilometers south of Nelspruit, South Africa. Their tips are consistent with the kind of tools that could have carved the petroglyphs. When they broke they were discarded, as could be the case with these tools. The patina on these discarded tools suggests that they were not used for well over 50,000 years.*

■ *Count the circles. A view of the mountains near Rustenburg, South Africa. This is another small example of the continuous stone settlements that once covered the entire southern African region. The road channels that once connected them can only be seen on close inspection of the enlarged image.*

But sometimes the data just does not fit the pet theory. According to the Bible, the first humans on Earth must have already had iron tools, because Adam, Cain, and Abel used iron tools to work their fields. It also suggests that the first humans knew the art of agriculture.

The start of the Bronze Age is another problem. The conventional belief of when the use of bronze first emerged lies somewhere between 2500 and 2000 BC. This would have caused a big problem for the builders of the first Egyptian pyramids, because they did not have metals hard enough to carve the giant stones. They did, however, have large supplies of copper and gold.

■ *A spectacular example of a dry stone wall near Waterval Boven, South Africa*

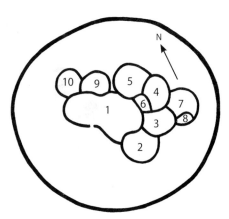

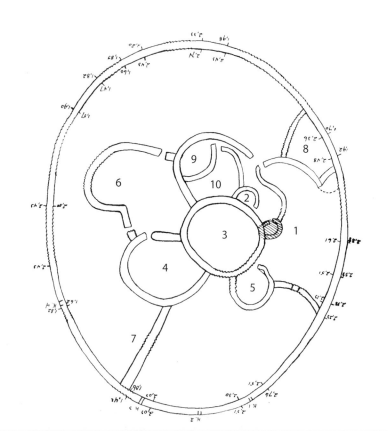

■ *Archaeological sketches of large stone ruins from 1939. The one on the left was the larger of the two, which was completely destroyed by the building of the N4 highway—a great tragedy indeed. Once again, the immediate curiosity is that there were no entrances in the original constructions.*

■ *An aerial view of the ruin as it looks today*

We are told that they achieved all those marvels of construction with copper tools. We all know that copper and gold will not carve any stone. What becomes evident is that those so-called early primitive humans had a lust for gold long before they felt the need for the much harder and useful metals like bronze and iron.

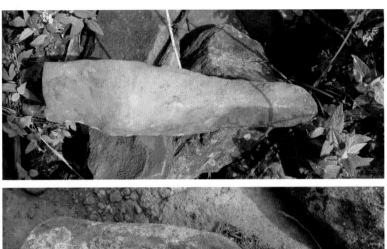

■ *A few examples of pointed stone tools. This is a very common shape of tools found virtually at every ruin.*

This is what I found in British history books about bronze and the curious obsession with gold:

At the end of the Neolithic period, around 4000 years ago [2000 BC], there was a people who arrived in Britain that we now call "Beaker," after the distinctive pottery that they were buried with. These people brought with them the skill and knowledge of producing and using bronze. Up to then, the only metal in use was gold, which is all right for decoration, but not hard enough for anything else. Bronze was a metal hard enough to hold an edge, and that meant a revolution in tools and weapons.

Our teachers have always assumed that gold was used for decoration. This is a very naive outlook and is suggested only by those who have not been exposed to the true properties of gold as a power and healing source. So, with all the gold in the world, it took another 1,000 years for iron to arrive in Britain. Can you see the immediate problem here? According to the conventional time line of metals arriving in certain parts of the world, Stonehenge could not have been built before 2500 BC, because they did not have metal tools hard enough to carve the stones. Once you start researching this phenomenon you soon realize that the mining of metals in southern Africa has a much earlier history—and the evidence is there to support it.

The Sumerian tablets tell us that the ancient people of the ABZU were mining all kinds of minerals many thousands of years ago, long before conventional archaeology seems to suggest. I have accumulated many stone tool anomalies that were either carved with metal tools or shaped with other forms of more advanced technology—like sound and resonance—the way Keely showed us in 1888. Archaeological evaluation suggests that these stone tools could be 50,000 years old or even much older. This poses a real problem for our current view of history, because humans were not supposed to have had any metal tools 50,000 years ago.

In the spring of 2004 the *Edinburgh Geologist* website printed an article that relates to ancient mining in southern Africa. This is an extract from the article.

When prospecting operations were carried out in 1957 in an area known as the Bomvu Ridge in the Ngwenya massif of Swaziland they estimated some 30,000,000 tons of iron with a mean value of 60% metallic iron content. The Swaziland Iron Ore Devoudment Corporation decided to mine the ore body and production started in 1964. The ore was taken

■ *Ngwenya iron mine in Swaziland*

by rail to the port of Maputo in Mozambique and from there shipped to Japan.

During the mining so many ancient stone tools were found that the news reached the archaeologist Professor Raymond Dart in South Africa. Dart sent a knowledgeable colleague called Adrien Boshier to investigate these finds and report back. What Boshier found was amazing, specialised stone tools made of dolerite, which is not a local stone, had been left behind by the early miners. These choppers, picks and hammerstones were not just on the surface but also deep underground. It seems that these early miners removed at least 1,200 tons of soft haematite ore rich in specularite from one particular mine, Lion Cavern, alone.

The question was how old were these mines? Archaeologist Peter Beaumont was producing evidence which suggested that these mines had

■ *The author in the oldest part of the Ngwenya mine, Lion's Cavern. This is the oldest recognized mine in the world, dating back as far as 100,000 years ago—and yet there are still those who continue to deny the evidence of ancient mining.*

been operated in the Iron Age, Late Stone Age and possibly even Middle Stone Age. However, hard evidence was still required in order to put a more precise date on the ancient mines. Then in 1967 charcoal nodules from some of the more ancient adits were sent to Yale and Groningen universities for Carbon 14 testing. The results that came back were astounding, dates of around 41,000 to 43,000 were obtained. Later from another early mine complex the buried skeleton of a child was dated at over 50,000 years.

Other archaeologists and anthropologists have suggested that these ancient mines must be much older simply based on the style of tools, artifacts, and the presence of human remains. They have suggested a date of more than 100,000 years old. The signs are quite clear that iron ore has been mined for more than 100,000 years in southern Africa, but this information has been buried. Could it be because it does not fit the mainstream theories of human evolution?

■ *Perfectly carved holes in rocks. Many of these show metallic residue around the edges, as if they were used as crucibles for molten metals.*

In 1973 *Reader's Digest* published a detailed article about the ancient mines in southern Africa. This is a short extract to further highlight these ancient mines.

Beaumont was engaged to explore the site with Boshier. In 18 months the young researchers located ten ancient filled-in pits, some as deep as 45 feet, from which a bright-red ore called hematite had been dug. In these pits were some of the richest deposits of Stone Age relics ever uncovered, including thousands of cleavers, picks, hammers, wedges and chisels, heavily bruised from use. From archaeological and geologic evidence, the earliest strata have been estimated to be 70,000 to 80,000 years old . . .

Having discovered the reason for the mines, Boshier and Beaumont began to look for the miners. It was this quest that led them to start digging at Border Cave. The cave had been investigated in 1934, and scientists had found various pieces of fossilized human skull and bone there, including the infant skeleton lying in a shallow grave in a Middle Stone Age stratum. But since radiocarbon dating had not yet been developed and the bones were of modern type, they evoked little interest. The earth of the grotto had remained undisturbed for 30 years when Boshier and Beaumont plunged their trowels into it in December 1970. In 50 active days, before supplies and money ran out, they unearthed some 300,000 artifacts and charred animal bones, many of creatures long extinct. Charcoal from an overlying ash level, more recent than the stratum in which the child's skeleton was discovered, proved to exceed the limit of radiocarbon dating, which is around 50,000 years. Thus the burial had occurred more than 50,000 years ago, but exactly how much earlier is difficult to say. Stone implements and ground ochre appear right down to bedrock, nine feet below the surface, suggesting that the cavern had been occupied for the last 100,000 years. "Practically everything we found was three times older than the books said it should have been," Boshier observes.

It is commonly believed that people in the early and middle Stone Age did not build circular stone structures. This is also a misconception. If only mainstream archaeologists took the time to excavate the well-known site of Melville Koppies, Johannesburg, they would be surprised to find that the foundations were originally laid by Stone Age settlers. In Wolmeransstad, I discovered Stone Age tools in an ancient circular stone ruin, which is part of a larger stone settlement. The incredible thing is that the stone axes from these stone ruins have been dated to be between 200,000 and 400,000 years old.

In the same settlement I found the remains of mud hut walls that cannot be older than 300 years. This simply indicates how civilizations build on top of each other or simply reinhabit existing structures. At this particular site there is overwhelming evidence of continued human habitation for several hundred thousand years. Near Rustenburg there are stone ruins that have been estimated to be about 18,000 years old and which display signs of agriculture and the probable presence of an extinct domesticated animal called the fat-tailed sheep. The same can be said for the ruins at Waterval Boven, where Stone Age tools dating to for more than 200,000 years ago have been found near pottery dating to around the 1600s.

In the same *Reader's Digest* article, Boshier and Beaumont continue with the following statement:

> [A]s early as 100,000 years ago man had developed an interest in happenings beyond the needs of survival. He had begun to question the purpose of existence and the nature of human destiny, to seek causes and fabricate explanations. This was the birth of intellect and the ascendancy of reason . . . It may be years before prehistorians can fully evaluate the significance of these . . . discoveries, but from the evidence it seems clear that modern man evolved on earth far earlier than has been realized and that most probably it was in the darkness of an African cave that the miracle of civilization had its genesis.

■ *A larger cavity in a rock with distinct metallic residue around the rim of the hollowed section. I have found several such examples.*

■ Strange stone tool/object found inside a stone circle ruin near Koster, South Africa.

■ A strange tool found on a terrace near Waterval Boven, estimated to be at least 50,000 years old.

■ The largest grindstone I have found to date. It is about 1.5 meters long and close to a meter wide. Tools like these should be smooth on the inside grinding surface. The erosion patterns inside this one suggest that it has not been used for well over 100,000 years.

■ Holes carved in a flat triangular rock are not just random holes but could well be an intricate sundial as indicated by Professor Pieter Wagener and photographed by Brenda Sullivan, author of Spirit of the Stones.

So what was going on here for so long? What was the main attraction that kept people so busy, in this part of the world, for several hundred thousand years? GOLD!

Quest for Gold

■ One of many ancient gold mines the author visited. This one is near Lydenburg, South Africa.

WHEN FERNANDES LEFT the port of Sofala, Mozambique in AD 1510, his instructions were clear and simple—find the kings of the fabled Monomotapa and find the gold of the land. The gold was no fable: I visited dozens of gold mines with Marius Brits. Marius is a researcher and explorer of note in the Lydenburg area who has a stunning collection of photographs to support his work and an intricate knowledge of ancient southern African sites. The current belief is that these gold mines were first mined during the 1880s gold rush. We have a very different take on this tale. It is no coincidence that wherever you find old gold mines there are always remains of ancient stone circles, terraces, and signs of lost civilizations who mined gold here long before anyone else. It is more likely that the prospectors in the late 1800s found the ancient gold mines near the stone circles and realized that wherever there are circles, there is gold. A good argument for this is that many of these mines are high up against the mountains, near stone circles—not the normal place you would find gold mines.

Since the time of Fernandes, the scramble for Africa by the colonialists has pretty much revolved around gold and other precious minerals in the ground. Somehow the ancient inhabitants in Africa knew how to extract gold and have been doing so for thousands of years. The learned Moors who tried to make sense of the ruins in Zimbabwe around 1552 believed that the stone structures were "very ancient" and were constructed to keep control and possession of the gold mines. Thousands of ancient gold mines have been reported over the past few centuries, and I have identified several dozen more.

The Portuguese were beaten to the gold rush by a few others before them. Egyptian pharaoh Rameses the Great, around 1300 BC, is said to have crossed the African continent to the southern tip in search of gold and then sailed beyond to Antarctica. Roman emperor Antoninus Pius controlled gold-digging operations here in AD 138. Arab records show that Arabic traders were already doing trade with southern Africa since around AD 800. And let's not forget the Indian gold merchants, the MaKomates, who traded gold from southern Africa, possibly as far back as 2000 BC.

If the Sumerian texts are correct in their description of ancient gold mines in southern Africa as far back as 280,000 years ago, it makes absolutely perfect sense as to where King Solomon got all his gold. By the time he came to power he must have obtained his gold from a place with a long and established history of gold mining. Solomon lived around 1000 BC, and according to texts he accumulated more wealth than any other king before him. The mysterious biblical Land of Ophir takes on a whole new meaning, and there can be no doubt where most of the gold originated in those early days. Southern Africa is the place where most of the gold in the world has been mined in modern history, and it was no different in ancient times.

■ *This Roman coin of Antoninus Pius, who ruled Rome from AD 138, was found by Theodore Bent about 25 meters deep in a gold mine near Mutare, Zimbabwe—a crucial bit of information that was conveniently misplaced. The Romans were here mining gold or trading in gold at the same time as the Dravidians, who were discussed in more detail in the chapter "Obsession with the Stars," page 52.*

■ Terraces and at least eight stone circles near Lydenburg. They are covered by soil and grass and are set only in this small section of the mountain, surrounded by hundreds of ancient gold mines that were reused by the prospectors of the 1800s. Once prospectors knew that the ancient mines were associated with the circles, it became a stampede to find the next ancient mine and claim it.

■ Some of the mines were barricaded by the last miners to prevent scavengers dipping into their golden ore. It does not seem that it really worked.

■ *A few more examples of the dozens of deserted mines high up against the mountain.*

Is it a coincidence that arguably the richest gold mine in the world today, Sheba Gold Mine, is located a few miles from Adam's Calendar in Mpumalanga, South Africa? These may seem like naive questions to some, but after witnessing the enormous ancient cities and civilizations in southern Africa myself, I am convinced that what we think we know about our ancient human history is further from the truth than we have ever imagined. It is also important to note that the word *Ophir* stems from the ancient Near Eastern name for Africa, which was "Afir" or "Aphir." This later led to the people of Africa being referred

■ *The author shows the proportions of the mine tunnel. It was not a pleasant task to cart the ore out of there. Notice the orbs floating around him.*

■ *Another mine entrance with unknown depth*

to as "K'Afir," and this led to the similar-sounding and very offensive South African expression for black people. Right next to Sheba Gold Mine we recently discovered three ancient gold mines, one of them being probably more than 100 meters deep. These lie right on the edge of a completely ruined stone settlement, which covers the entire hill.

■ *Examples of two well-preserved stone circles. The larger one has several large stones built into the walls. The author does not have any theories on this as yet, but based on the high content of quartz it could have aided in the process of conducting and generating energy.*

The images on pages 146–47 show how small the entrances to the mine tunnels were. Mining was no easy job, no matter the era. Perhaps there is still energetic residue from the difficulties the generations of miners faced. In the image on page 149, notice the light-colored spheres against the dark background of the tunnel. These are orbs. For those who are new to the orb phenomenon—these are nonphysical energies in spherical form and many different sizes. Some believe that they are disembodied souls. The brilliant theologian and scholar of note Miceal Ledwith has done extensive research on the orb spheres, and actual energy readings were measured. Digital cameras pick them up because of their ability to capture

■ *The remains of the hoist house from the late 1800s mining activities. A cable ran down to the valley near the river where the ore was crushed and processed.*

■ *A spectacular picture of a mine shaft filled with so many orbs that we can hardly see the passage.*

infrared and ultraviolet parts of the light spectrum. Most people cannot see orbs unaided, but some people are able to see them with the naked eye. This could be evidence of retinal evolution taking place, or simply the rise of consciousness. Are the orbs in these mines souls of the dead miners, or new inquisitive ones feeding on the energy of the past?

■ Two great examples of ancient gold mines going straight down into the ground. The holes are very deep, probably more than 100 meters. There are no records of these mines, and somehow they slipped through the fingers of the mining giants. Not surprisingly, they are close to the richest gold mine in the world today—Sheba Gold Mine.

■ *A road cuts right through the center of a stone circle. The strata is spectacular—showing all kinds of anomalous tools, and even ash from unknown activity.*

■ *Five-meter high strata along a road shows sediment and deposits of stones and monoliths from stone walls of ancient ruins.*

■ *Just one of thousands of anomalous tools washed into the road high up against the mountain.*

■ *The author sits dangerously close to the edge of a deep mine shaft.*

■ *Strangely shaped and carved stones lie scattered among the many stone circles that surround the mine shaft.*

■ *A snap shot of the shaft itself. It is probably more than 100 meters deep, and it may even have side shafts splitting away from the main vertical.*

■ *Johan Heine examines the entrance to an ancient gold mine high on a mountain in Mpumalanga, South Africa.*

■ *The author points out the remains of a stone circle wall, which was part of a large settlement all around the deep mine shaft. Note the distinct shape of one of Adam's Pyramids in the background. Always close to the gold—in antiquity and in modern times too.*

Sumerian Tablets

AN ARTICLE BY Faye Flam in the July 24, 2002, edition of the *Philadelphia Inquirer* states:

> The people known as Sumerians are credited with starting the first civilization and building the first settlements worthy of being called cities. They also invented writing, and then they wrote and wrote and wrote, filling millions of tablets with their intricate, detailed characters. They left behind everything from religious texts to poetry to receipts, much of which remains preserved 5,000 years later . . . The Sumerians settled and farmed the area between the Tigris and Euphrates Rivers in Mesopotamia, now part of Iraq. Around 3500 B.C., they became the first people on Earth to congregate in cities, to use complex mathematics, and to record their ideas with a written language. They did most of their writing between 3000 and 2000 B.C. Over the next millennium, they were gradually assimilated into the Babylonian civilization, which continued to advance Sumerian literature, astronomy, and mathematics.

For people who study religious texts it is critical to note that much of what we read in the Bible has been taken and adapted from thousands of Sumerian clay tablets. These tablets have slowly and systematically been deciphered over the past 150 years by a growing number of scholars. Today some universities have established Sumerian translation departments and employ advanced computer programs to scan and translate these clay tablets. It was only in the past forty years, however, that the true meaning of these translations started to play havoc with our perception of human history. It is commonly accepted by scholars that we have inherited almost everything we know from the Sumerians: the wheel, writing, medicine, astronomy, architecture, agriculture, geometry, mathematics, the law, and much more. It was the crafty Sumerians who first developed and applied these disciplines. As discussed in the chapter "Human

Origins and Mythology" (page 22) this early civilization also had their pantheon of twelve gods who ruled their lives, rewarded them, and punished them if they stepped out of line and were the first holy trinity—consisting of the gods Anu, Enlil, and Enki.

The Sumerians built impressive temples to these gods and had many personal and physical encounters with them, just like many of the biblical characters had with the God of the Old Testament. It is important to note that these were the first gods in recorded human history who expressed their obsession with gold and made it clear that all the gold of the planet belonged to them. It was this same message that was passed on to the Spanish conquistadores when they began to terrorize the Native American people. The Spaniards came across unthinkable amounts of stored gold, gold artifacts, and entire golden cities. They were told unequivocally by the Native Americans that "all the gold belongs to the gods."

■ *This is MS 2855 of the Schøyen Collection in the Oslo museum. It is one of only six clay tablets in existence that actually name the pre-Flood kings who ruled the world over a total period of 222,600 years. Two of the tablets give exactly the same information, while the others have slight deviations. The actual translation is this:*

List of kings and cities from before the Flood in Eridu: Alulim ruled as king 28,800 years. Elalgar ruled 43,200 years. Eridu was abandoned. Kingship was taken to Bad-Tibira. Ammilu'anna the king ruled 36,000 years. Enmegalanna ruled 28,800 years. Dumuzi ruled 28,800 years. Bad-Tibira was abandoned. Kingship was taken to Larak. En-sipa-zi-anna ruled 13,800 years. Larak was abandoned. Kingship was taken to Sippar. Meduranki ruled 7,200 years. Sippar was abandoned. Kingship was taken to Shuruppak. Ubur-tutu ruled 36,000 years. Total: 8 kings; their years: 222,600.

As the Flay article mentioned, one thing the Sumerians did really well was to capture their activities on clay tablets. They covered everything: the first calendar, poetry, recipes, court proceedings, music, and especially their history and tales of their origins—which included the creation of Earth and the solar system in a group of tablets called the *Enuma Elish,* or *Epic of Creation.* The Sumerians explain in great detail how man was created, and how the gods made him in their image with the single purpose to toil in the gold mines of the ABZU. It also explains how Lord Enki, who was in charge of the gold mining, chose his domain and built a strong fortress in the ABZU, which is somewhere in modern-day Zimbabwe.

■ (left) MS 3026: Sumerian Flood Story. The story of the Great Flood as told by the Sumerians. This tablet introduces Ziusudra, the Sumerian Noah, and the events that led to the world being destroyed in a great flood of water.

■ (right) The Sumerian King List tablet, one of the most famous Sumerian tablets. It lists 149 kings and rulers on planet Earth, before and after the Flood. It outlines when the kingdom was lowered to Earth from heaven by the Anunnaki, or biblical Nephilim. The list also outlines the coming to Earth of the biblical Anakim. It describes how Ninurta—the youngest son of Enlil— the biblical Yahweh, destroyed Sodom and Gomorrah. This event was captured in great detail in another collection of tablets called the Erra Epos.

This description in the *Lost Book of Enki*, by Zecharia Sitchin, matches the profile of the Great Zimbabwe ruins perfectly and is one of the many Sumerian translations referring to mining activity in ancient times and the fate of modern humans.

"Great rivers there rapidly flowed. An abode by the flowing waters Enki for himself established." He established a fortress for his house and other places where the workers would live and "where the bowels of the Earth to enter . . . Place of deepness he determined, for the heroes into Earth's bowels to descend" to extract the gold.

Could these ancient stone ruins be the settlements of the early humans enslaved to work in ancient gold mines? Could the ancient Adam's Calendar at Kaapschehoop in Mpumalanga, South Africa, be the centerpiece of this era? Could some of the more elaborate and impressive ruins, like Great Zimbabwe, be the fortress remains of the ancient gods who controlled the gold-mining operations? These notions are not as crazy as they may seem at first glance.

We need to establish the levels of credibility of the Sumerian tablets and how far we are prepared to believe them. Thousands of scholars have gone to great lengths to show how accurate the Sumerian knowledge was. There is no suspicion among scholars that the information captured by the Sumerians was intended to deceive us, because we still apply much of their knowledge in our daily lives. What has become highly questionable is the selective approach taken by many scholars toward the content of the tablets. On the one hand we are taught how impressive the Sumerian civilization was and how accurate their science was, but in the same breath our historians tend to disregard all that was written by the same meticulous Sumerians about our human origins, God, Eden, Adam and Eve, and much of what we read in the Bible many thousands of years later. I struggle to understand why some scholars choose to disregard the information shared by the Sumerians about the early humans, the conditions they lived in, and their quest for gold in distant parts of the world. Once again it seems to be neglected simply because it does not fit their rosy model of human history.

Most of our Western history is based on Judeo-Christian religion and the early historians mostly fell into this category. While many of them have been exposed as being fraudulent, we still accept their viewpoints in our history books today and base our knowledge on those early fraudulent accounts. Some wrote with absolute certainty about events in the past, documenting fine details of who did what and who said what some 1,000 years after the event, as if they were there to witness it. These are the historic manuscripts upon which we base much of our perception of what happened in the past.

Here is a simple example of how one of the most famous historic figures was hijacked by historians of the past and remains entrapped in that character today. Remember that the biblical Gods (Elohim) interacted and communicated with the early people they had chosen. According to the Bible, Abraham was one such person. He traveled long and far guided by his God, crossing the whole of the Near East. He built a powerful army, because God gave him advanced weapons with which he could slay other armies many times the size of his. He also acquired immense wealth and controlled vast amounts of land given to him by God. Other rulers and kings feared him, because his God was more power-ful than theirs. Quite frankly the whole story of Abraham is highly suspicious, his activities defy any logic, and the destruction of Sodom and Gomorrah is a turning point in our Judeo-Christian past when compared to the Sumerian account of that important event.

After all, the Sumerians got their instructions and information from their gods, just like Abraham and Moses received information from their god. We should also remember that Abraham was not a Jew but a Sumerian from a town called Ur, and he features prominently in Sumerian history. So who was Abraham's god, and who were the Sumerian gods? They were the same group of deities described in detail in the Sumerian tablets and echoed in the Bible some 2,500 years later.

As far back as 1925 a *Nature* magazine article titled "The Indo-Sumerian Seals Deciphered: Discovering Sumerians of Indus Valley as Phoenicians, Barats, Goths and Famous Vedic Aryans, 3100–2300 BC" broke the story of irrefutable links between Sumerian and Indus Valley civilizations.

Col. Waddell, the well-known authority on Tibet, has stepped in where archaeologists, as yet, fear to tread. He has produced an interpretation of the remarkable seals which were found, with other relics suggesting an affinity with ancient Sumeria, at Mohenjo Daro and Harappa in the Indus Valley, and illustrated and described by Sir John Marshall, Director of the Archaeological Survey of India.

This is a crucial bit of information, because various scholars like Cyril Hromnik, Brenda Sullivan, and sangomas like Credo Mutwa have written in detail about the symbols that link the Sumerians with the Indus Valley, Egypt, and South Africa. The only mystery we need to resolve is the fact that the artifacts and petroglyphs in South Africa are many thousands of years older than any of the Northern Hemisphere civilizations.

■ *(opposite) A side view of the two main calendar stones of Adam's Calendar. It may be more accurate to call it Enki's Calendar, because as mentioned in the "Adam's Calendar" chapter (page 60) numerous psychics have independently confirmed that the Sumerian deity Enki was responsible for its construction. Notice the unusually thick lichen growth on the taller of the two monoliths, an indication of its true age. For those who are still skeptical about human psychic ability and scoff at such notions, I suggest you do some research into quantum physics, the vacuum, the nature of reality, and the morphogenic field that holds all universal knowledge embedded in it. This may lead you to come to grips with the natural ability of paranormal perception, or ESP, which all of us should be able to perceive—and yet for some reason we don't.*

The African-Sumerian Connection

■ *The original Sumerian winged disc was a simple cross in a circle with lines that represented wings attached to the sides. This evolved in various forms in the Near East and Egypt.*

■ *Another adaptation of the winged disc, this one showing a more advanced cross in the center. This image is seen in many Sumerian seals, often hovering above the subject.*

■ *A petroglyph of a winged disc in South Africa. This carving predates all those of northern civilizations and suggests that the origin of this symbol is also in southern Africa.*

IS IT POSSIBLE that the early Africans worshipped the same Sumerian gods many thousands of years before the Sumerians themselves? According to Credo Mutwa, that is exactly what happened. During September 2008 I visited Credo and his wife, Virginia, at their home. We spent most of the day exploring many issues, which included the murky origins of humankind, the lost civilizations of southern Africa, the importance of the sacred site we call Adam's Calendar, and many more fascinating topics that most people would probably frown at. During our chat Credo highlighted various important events for me.

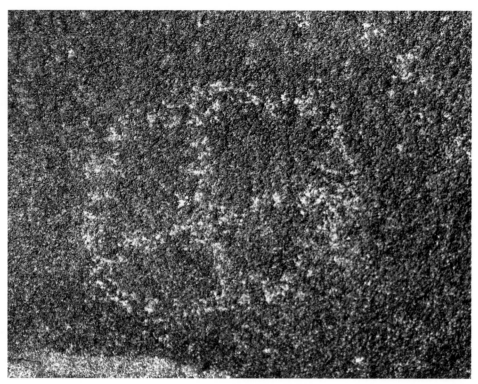

The most significant was that southern Africa is indeed the Cradle of Humankind. By this I do not mean the cradle of "hominid kind" as many scholars often suggest, but most certainly the cradle of modern humans—*Homo sapiens*—thinking man, the Sumerian Adamu or the biblical Adam. He also pointed out that this is the home of the original Abantu people, long before anyone had ever imagined. When Credo talks about the ancient Zulu, or African tradition/culture, he is actually referring to the FIRST people—the progenitors of all humans, the original Bantu—who lived long before the establishment of the many Bantu tribes as we know them today.

While modern historians tell us that the Bantu migrated to the south from northwest Africa starting some 2,000 years ago, our evidence shows that the ancestors and progenitors of the Bantu—the original humans—lived here long before that time. During various global disasters that spanned more than 60,000 years, those early humans migrated north, which is often called the "exodus from Africa." The most likely cause for this important event was the super-volcano that erupted at Lake Toba in Sumatra. This giant explosion was only recently detected by scientists, and they estimate that the prevailing winds carried most of the dust and poisonous gases westward toward eastern and southern Africa. All you need to do is look on a global map or Google Earth and you will quickly realize that there is very little in the path of the billions of tons of dust except the flat Indian ocean.

Scientists estimate that this eruption took place between 65,000 and 75,000 years ago. It was so massive that it would have caused a miniature ice age. The most affected areas would have been southern Africa, where the first civilization lived and functioned very successfully. This was most likely the trigger that caused the exodus of the FIRST people from southern Africa into the rest of the world. They took with them all their traditions and customs, which included the sacred symbols and imagery. For more than 200,000 years these FIRST people carved these images into stones and rock faces of the mountains of southern Africa. These included the many symbols that later emerged in the Egyptian and Sumerian civilizations, such as the winged planet/disc and the ankh. They took with them the knowledge of building with stone, which was refined over millennia in other parts of the world. We should therefore not be surprised when we find stone circle ruins all over the planet, because this was the most basic structure known to the FIRST people before they dispersed throughout the world.

Several thousand years later they started to migrate south to their original birthplace, possibly not even realizing that this is where they had initially come from.

Linda Tucker covers many more interesting aspects revealed to her by Credo Mutwa in her brilliant book *Children of the Sun God,* which includes the FIRST people and their place in human history, at the southern tip of Africa.

But who were the first and original Abantu people? Where did they get their name? Scholars have been arguing about the origins of the word *Bantu* or *Abantu* for decades. Some scholars like Cyril Hromnik suggest its origins lie in the Sanskrit word *bandhu,* meaning "brother, relative, kinsman." The bottom line is that there are no obvious answers but only speculation by various scholars, most of whom have not taken all the evidence into account. How could they? Until now it was thought that southern Africa was a barren land filled with a handful of hunter-gatherers who somehow survived for thousands of years. No one could have guessed that there are many lost cities covered by

■ *Some examples of the Indus Valley Script—as yet undeciphered. Close similarities can be found among the many petroglyphs in South Africa, but the South Africa petroglyphs are much older.*

■ *The Anglo-Saxon runes also show great similarities to the petroglyphs in South Africa and the Indus Script.*

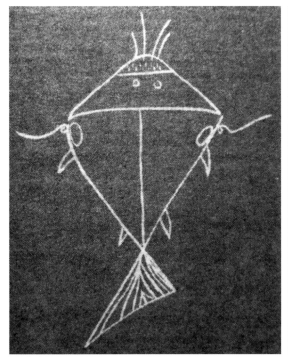 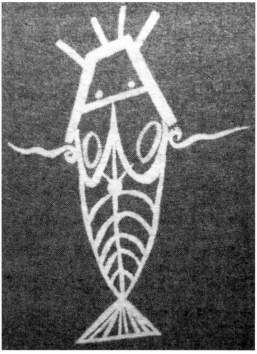

■ *Images show a Dogon drawing of a fish coming out of the water. It did not represent the simple act of fishing but something much more aligned with creation.*

■ *A seal with Indus Valley Script, as yet undeciphered. There are many similarities among the fish petroglyphs in South Africa and images used by both Dogon and Indus people. The South African petroglyphs are much older, however; probably more than 100,000 years old if judged by the erosion around the cracks through the glyphs.*

the sands of time, consisting of millions of ancient circular stone structures, all linked together by a mysterious grid of stone walls.

The root of the word *Abantu* is *ntu*. This little root has caused many heated debates in academic circles over the decades. The two places on Earth where this *ntu* root is most obviously found are in southern/eastern Africa and the ancient Sumerian civilization. Biblical historian and professor of theology Zecharia Sitchin devoted a lifetime of research to the Sumerians and the obscure origins of humankind. Sitchin's many books outline the pantheon of Sumerian gods, their relationships with each other, and their control of planet Earth in great detail. Therefore I was not surprised when Credo Mutwa launched into his own explanation regarding the source of the name Aba'ntu.

Credo describes how all the Sumerian gods had spouses or wives whose names often resembled those of the male gods. Enlil's spouse was Ninlil; Enki's wife was Ninki; and the wife of the supreme Sumerian god Anu was A'ntu. So now we come to realize that not only do the ancient symbols originate in southern Africa, but the first link to the ancient gods—who came to rule over the whole of the Near East many thousands of years later—comes from the Sumerian goddess A'ntu. Herein lies the link between all the ancient civilizations, starting with the FIRST people in southern Africa who worshipped a Sumerian goddess called A'ntu. It is astonishing to discover that ancient Zulu culture and religion, including those of all other Bantu tribes, is directly linked to the Sumerians. Credo concludes that *Abantu* is derived from the Sumerian goddess A'ntu, and Aba'ntu, and simply means "the children/people of A'ntu." A'ntu, the Sumerian goddess who loved the ABZU—where the gold came from.

Petroglyphs

■ *A small section of the large glaciated slabs of andesite rock at Driekopseiland near Kimberley, South Africa. There are thousands of glyphs on the slabs that cover about 3,000 square meters. There are staggering shapes and images of undeciphered scripts that seem to predate anything else on Earth.*

THE FOLLOWING IMAGES of petroglyphs are worth a thousand words. They show the connections between South African glyphs and Sumerian, Egyptian, and other advanced civilizations; the use of sacred geometry; the creation of sound energy; and the knowledge of time-keeping and the stars. The visual journey through these petroglyphs touches on all these topics, and more.

■ *Cross in a circle plus an oval shape dissected in half, near Carolina, South Africa.*

■ *Cross in a circle and the oval dissected at Driekopseiland, which shows that the same symbols were used across vast distances by ancient people in South Africa. The dissected oval is a representation of the moon goddess, while the cross in a circle represents the Lord of Light (Sullivan,* Spirit of the Rocks*).*

■ *Five distinctly different shapes indicating a consciously written script much earlier than any other script ever found. It shows great similarity to later Sumerian and Indus script and could even be the prototype for Chinese style of writing (Driekopseiland). The five-pointed star, as in the extreme left symbol, is also an Egyptian symbol of kingship associated with a link to the divine—specifically the god Baal.*

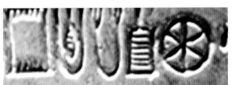

■ *Indus Script seal also showing a distinct star in a circle. The Sumerians also used an eight-pointed star in a circle as representation of the planet of the gods.*

■ *Sumerian seal showing a script similar to carvings at Driekopseiland, South Africa.*

■ *A cross—or possibly even an ankh—inside a hexagon, with concentric circles outward. This can be interpreted as quite a complex image involving the knowledge of matter, while the hexagon represents a star tetrahedron. The ankh is synonymous with sound frequency in the generation of energy, inside concentric circles as amplification chambers. This is basic knowledge of energy that we do not possess today. Once again the erosion indicates its extreme age of more than 100,000 years at least.*

■ *A very complex carving by a well-informed person, a long, long time ago. It depicts a serpent, representing vibrational frequency, or ohm shape (Ω)—also approximating the Om shape, inside a pentagon, with a star above it. The horseshoe shape is often depicted as one of the six syllables of Om. The Om is regarded as the prime sound of creation because of its vibrational frequency. The serpent has always been seen as the creator in most ancient cultures. The shape of the pentagon is associated with the creator because of the phi factor, or 1.618 ratio. The dot above the serpent could represent a star like Sirius, or another star associated with creation and worship among ancient African cultures. Similar horseshoe shapes are found among the ruins.*

■ *An ancient coin from Greece showing an identical serpent in the same horseshoe shape. The recurrence of this serpent shape and shapes among the ruins is not accidental but shows an understanding of sound and vibrational frequency.*

■ *Carvings in a cave in Limpopo
province, northern South Africa.
The cross is identical to Sumerian
crosses found in numerous
Sumerian seals.*

■ *Petroglyphs found near Lydenburg, South Africa. Note the perfectly drilled holes in very specific sequence, probably marking the movements of some stars or planets, or maybe the moon. It was probably a calendar of some kind. How they drilled the holes remains a mystery.*

■ *Driekopseiland*

■ *Mpuluzi, close to the Swaziland border*

■ *Lambda symbols scattered on rocks around South Africa are identical to those found in Anglo-Saxon runes and Indus Script. The symbol is not yet understood, but its appearance at locations separated by vast distances indicates that the symbol carried an important meaning.*

■ *Wolmeransstad*

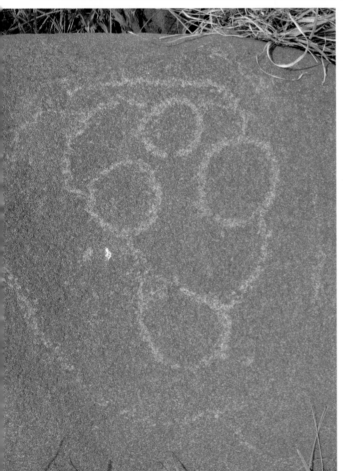

■ *A rhino carving at Wildebeeskuil, South Africa. The cracks through the carving once again indicate that it is much older than the 2,000 years ascribed to it.*

■ *More petroglyphs of circular structures, Carolina.*

■ *Wave forms like these are associated with water and life, but they could also represent the knowledge of frequency and its application as the primary source of energy—whether it was from the sun or emanating from Mother Earth.*

■ *Two examples of the same image from different locations. They are very similar to the Dogon people's images of the seed of life, the germination of matter, or creation, indicated by the incomplete circle and the rays of energy emanating from it.*

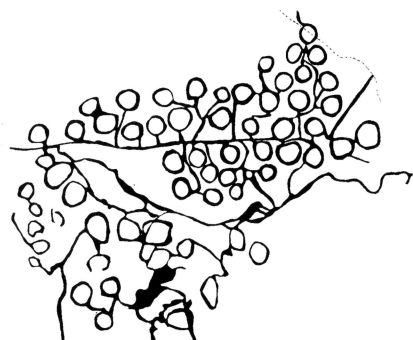

■ *Carving of a stone circle complex near Waterval Boven. It is very similar to the archaeological sketches from Nooitgedacht Dam, resembling a cluster of grapes. Note the absence of entrances. The circles are all joined together by channels, or roads. Now that we understand the energy-generating principle, it seems that this is a good example of an early diagram of an energy-generating complex. The energy flows via the channels that connect them all together to create a continuous energy grid. The simple, nonpolar (or radiant) energy would have been used for everything as we imagine it today—and more. It is not a dangerous form of energy like the polar electricity we use today.*

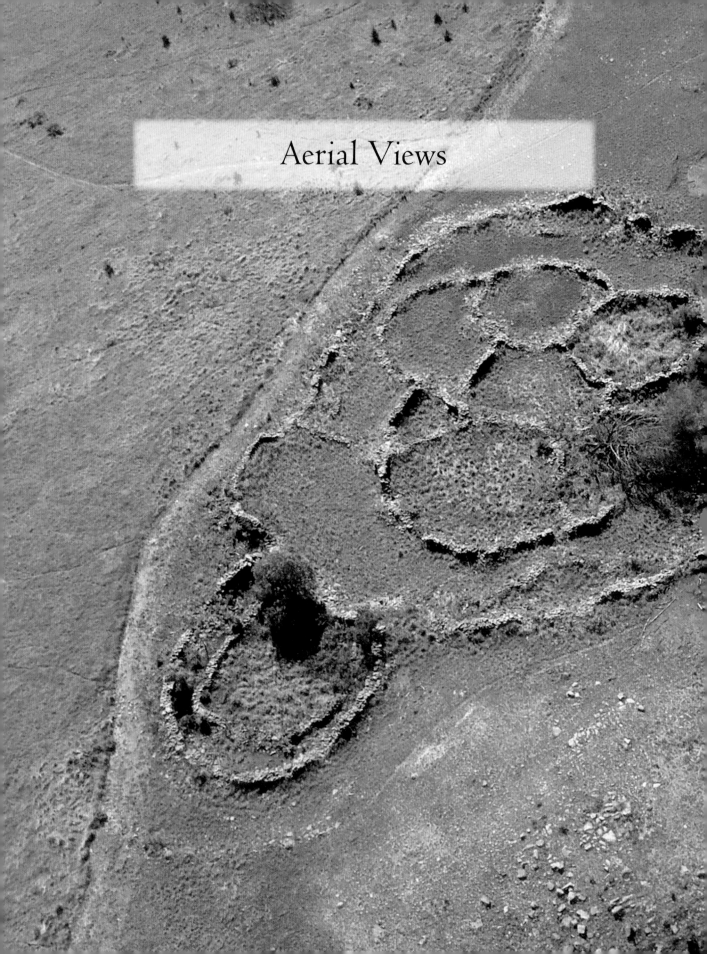

Aerial Views

■ *One of the largest ruins the author has been researching. It measures 150 meters across. The only entrance to the structure seems to be created by later inhabitants.*

WHAT FOLLOWS IN this chapter is a stunning aerial voyage over these mysterious ruins. The majesty of these structures can only be experienced from the air. From this perspective questions are both answered and raised. The journey, however, is always astounding.

■ *The extended web that once connected all these ruins is now not visible and well covered by soil and grass. Note the horseshoe, ohmlike shape that faces the spiral of the large ruin—suggesting once again the manipulation of sound and energy.*

■ *Thousands of ruins are in forestry areas, well out of sight. Many thousands have been destroyed and continue to be destroyed. Sappi, Ltd., a global paper company that has pulp and timber operations in this region of southern Africa, has become aware of its impact on the ruins and is involved with the MaKomati Foundation to protect and clear some of the more accessible and prominent stone structures. Unfortunately this is not enough and they need to do much more to make up for their destruction of many thousands of ancient sites. The author's attempts to get them involved in any kind of research and support have failed. The Komatiland forestry company, which manages the land where Adam's Calendar stands, has actively tried many tricks to prevent the author from entering the area. The same goes for the government of South Africa through the Department of Water and Forestry. They keep trying everything to keep people out of the area and away from the calendar—even though it has not been acknowledged as an ancient site by the government. They still view it as a bunch of random rocks.*

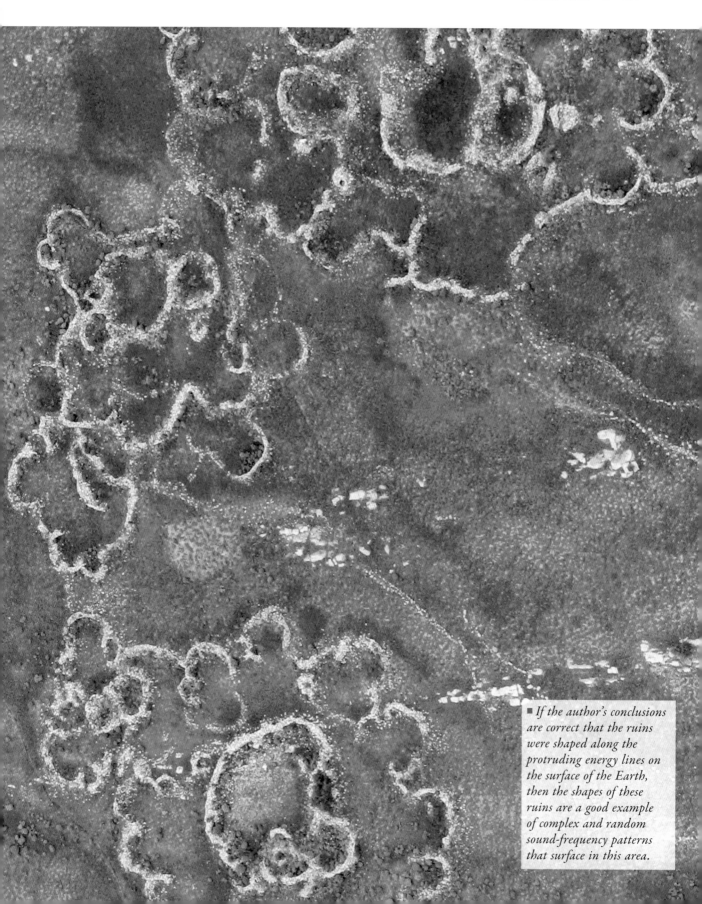

■ If the author's conclusions are correct that the ruins were shaped along the protruding energy lines on the surface of the Earth, then the shapes of these ruins are a good example of complex and random sound-frequency patterns that surface in this area.

■ *Notice the concentric circles, probably acting as resonant amplification, and the extended web of walls that surrounds the central circle.*

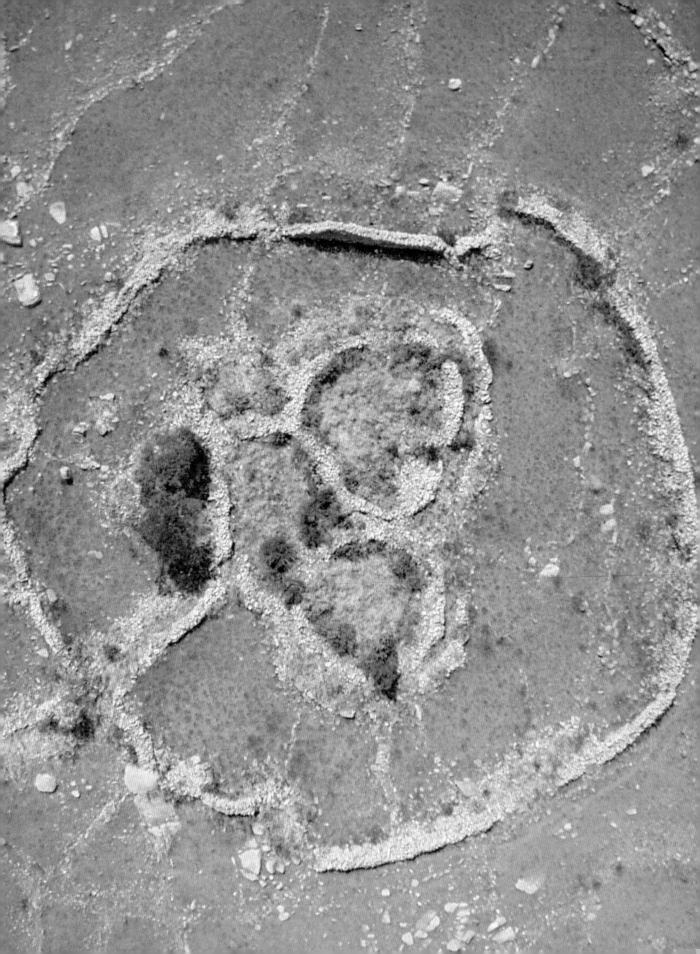

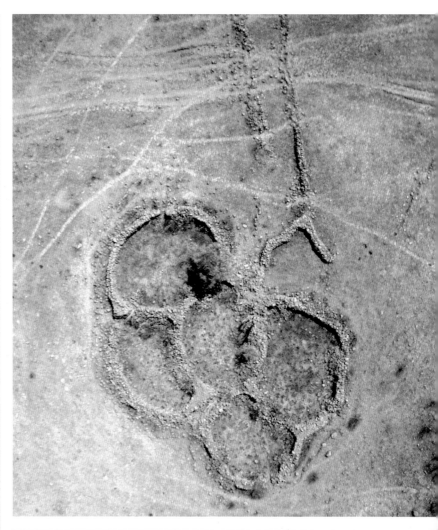

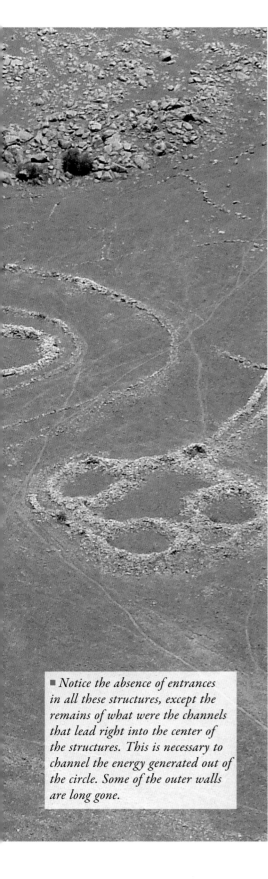

■ *Notice the absence of entrances in all these structures, except the remains of what were the channels that lead right into the center of the structures. This is necessary to channel the energy generated out of the circle. Some of the outer walls are long gone.*

■ *An example of stone circles with an existing outer wall. The weblike pattern around the entire structure is visible.*

■ *More examples of stone circles and outer walls*

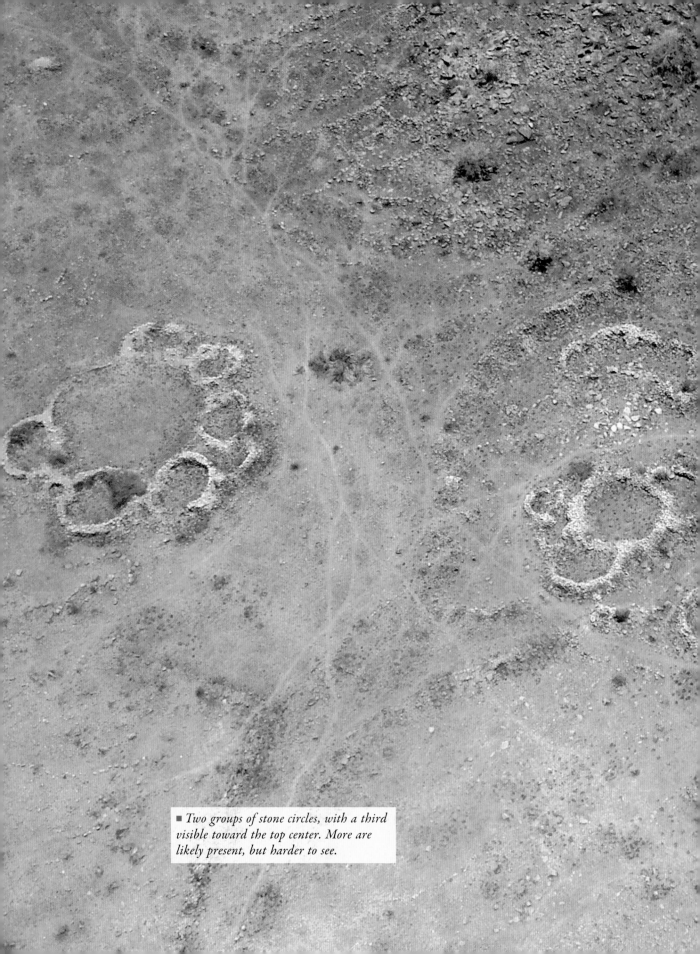

■ *Two groups of stone circles, with a third visible toward the top center. More are likely present, but harder to see.*

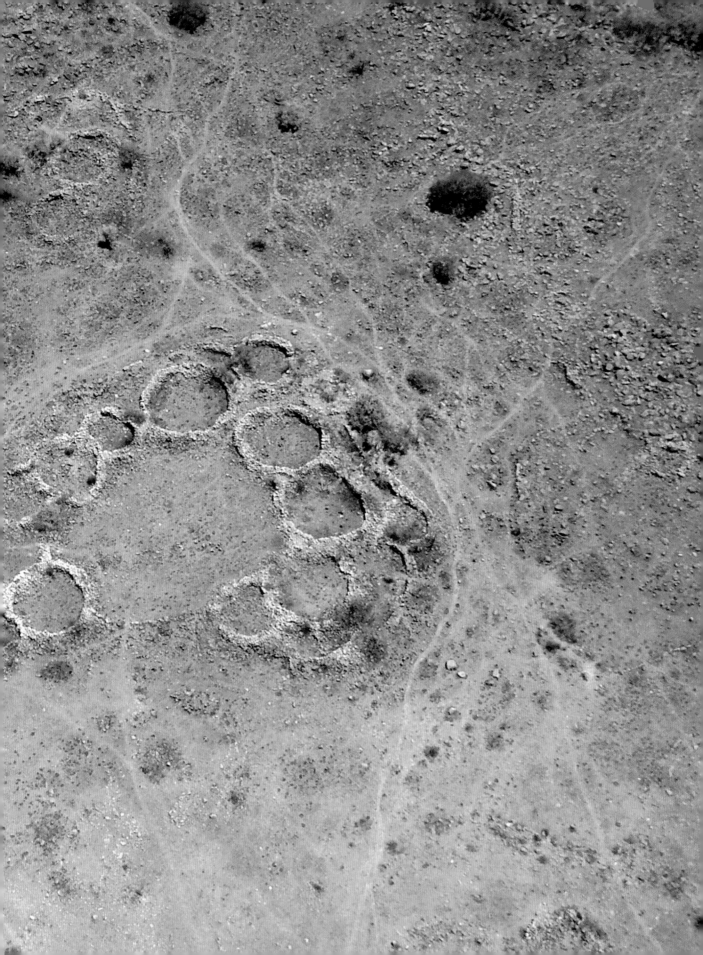

■ *Stone circle with radiating pattern evident in the terrain*

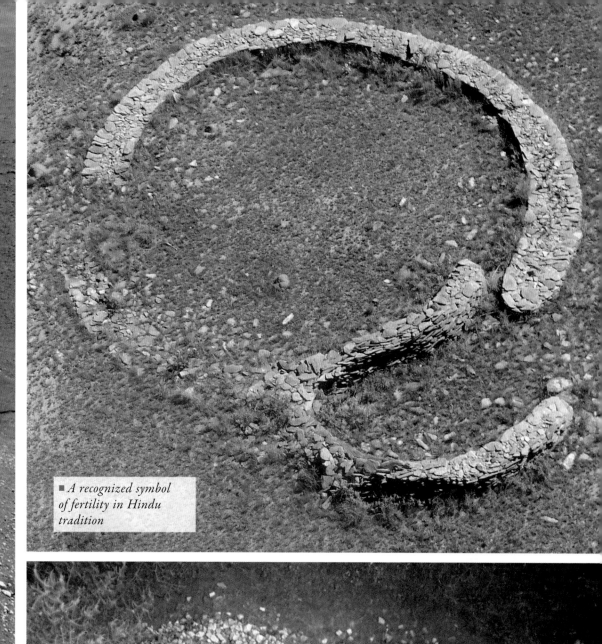

■ *A recognized symbol
of fertility in Hindu
tradition*

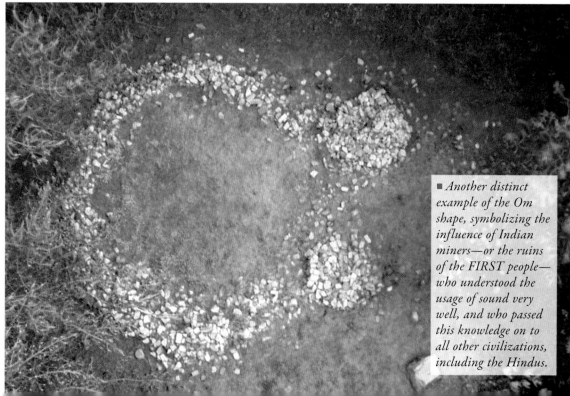

■ *Another distinct
example of the Om
shape, symbolizing the
influence of Indian
miners—or the ruins
of the FIRST people—
who understood the
usage of sound very
well, and who passed
this knowledge on to
all other civilizations,
including the Hindus.*

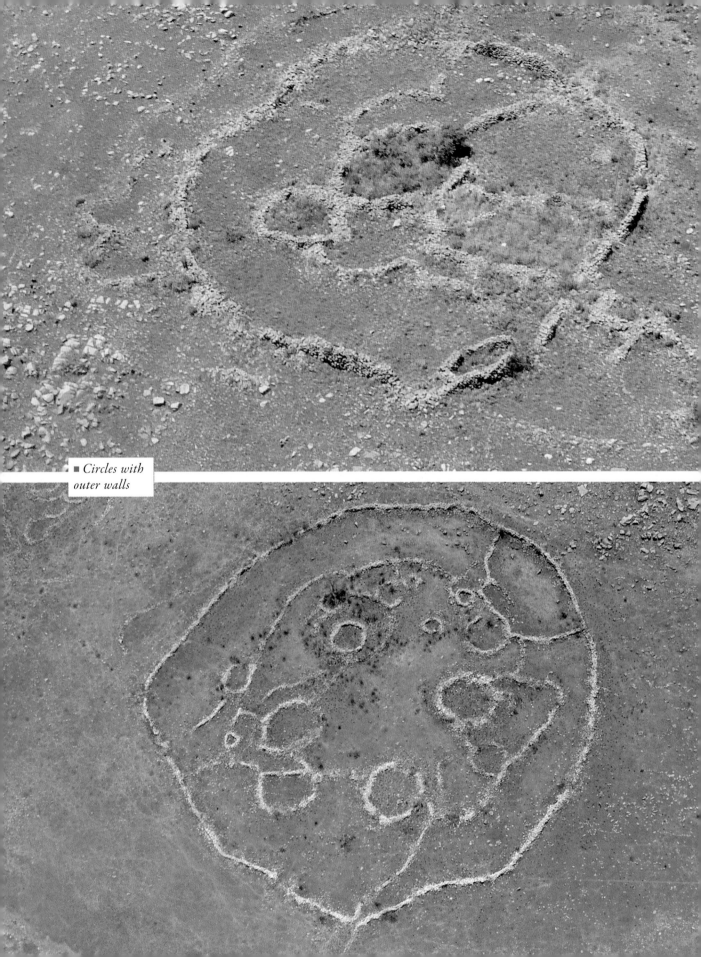

■ *Circles with outer walls*

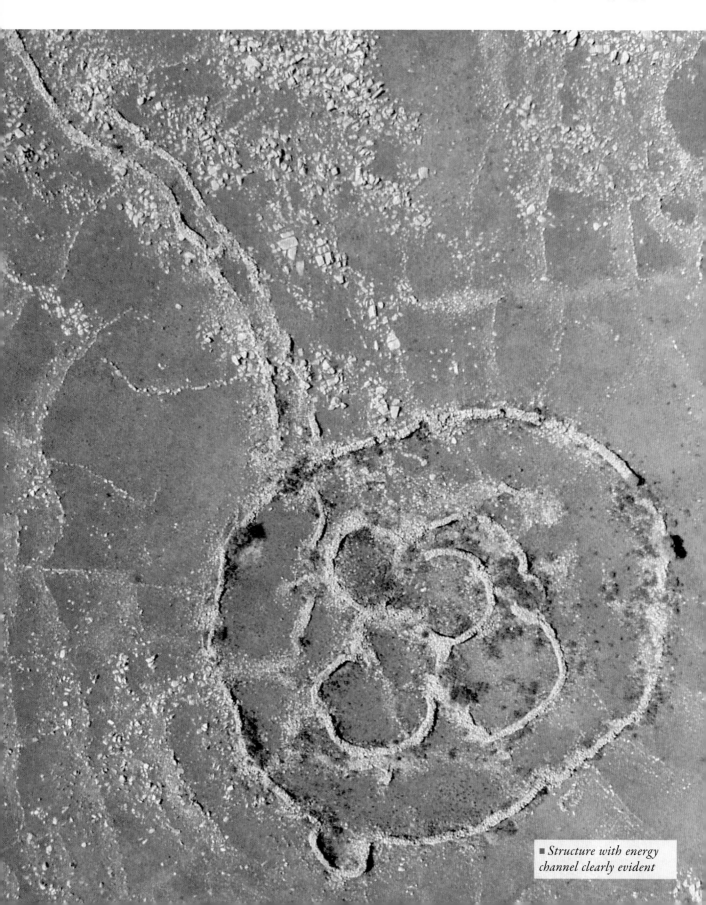

■ *Structure with energy channel clearly evident*

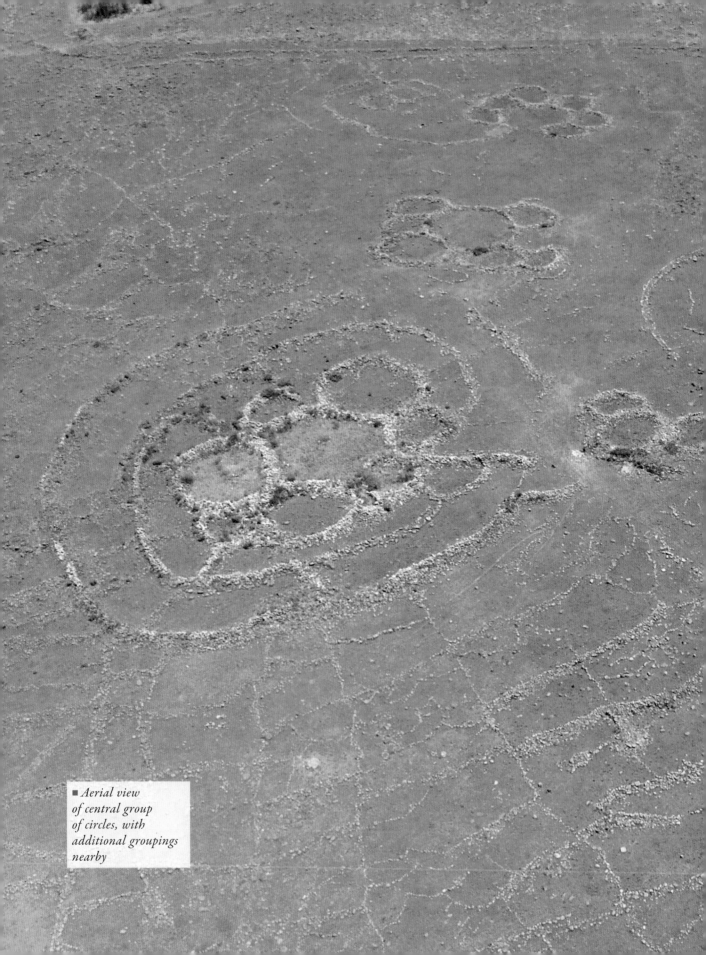

■ *Aerial view of central group of circles, with additional groupings nearby*

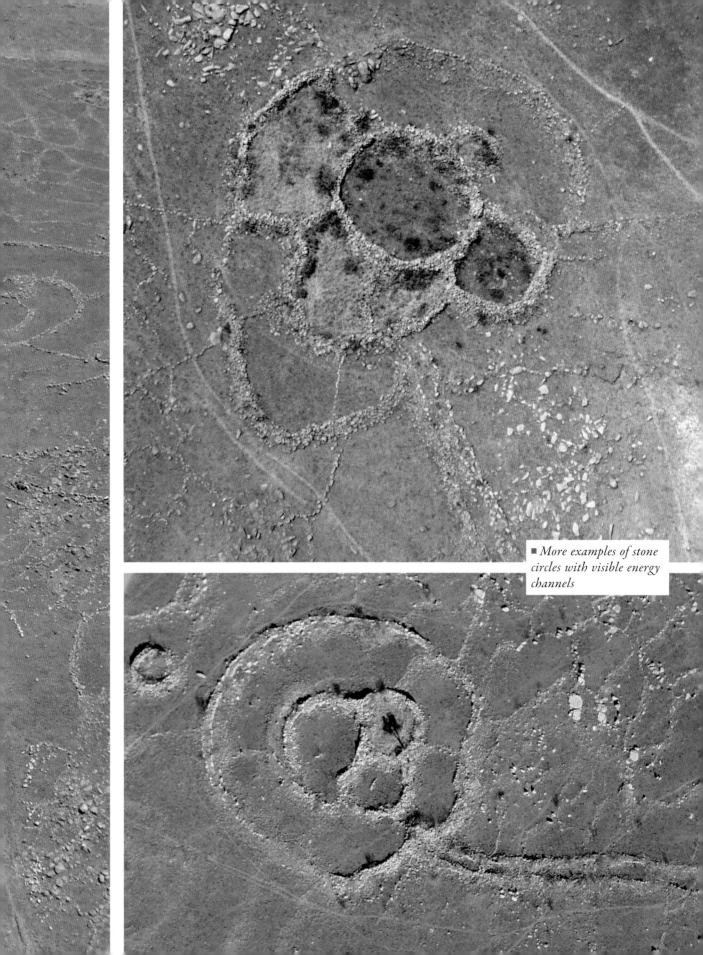

■ *More examples of stone circles with visible energy channels*

■ *Stone circles with outer wall, and rocks scattering the landscape*

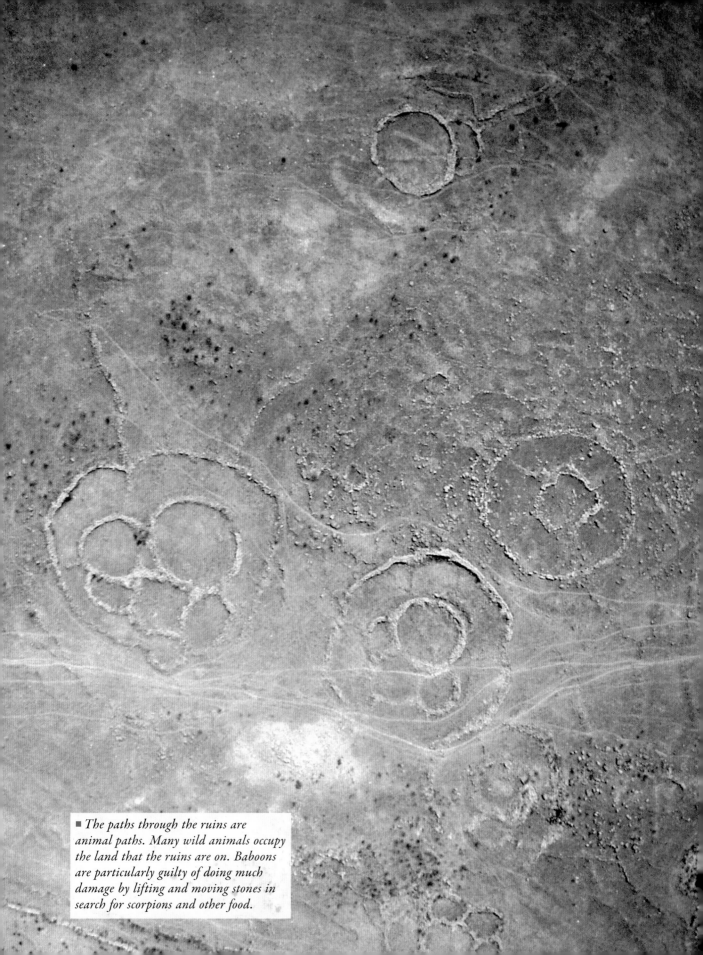

■ *The paths through the ruins are animal paths. Many wild animals occupy the land that the ruins are on. Baboons are particularly guilty of doing much damage by lifting and moving stones in search for scorpions and other food.*

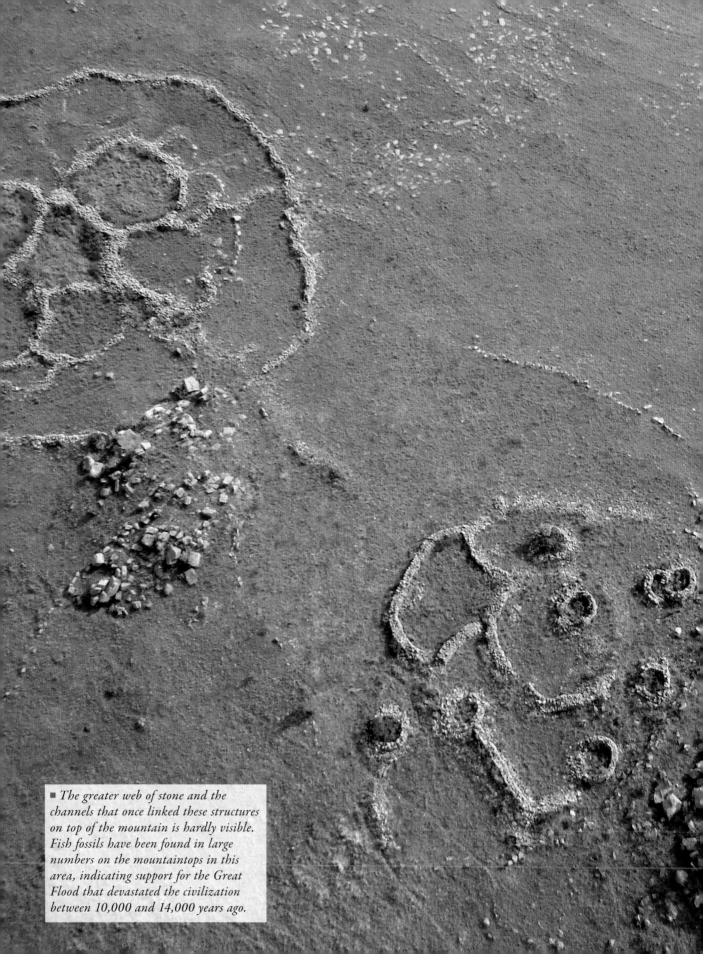

■ *The greater web of stone and the channels that once linked these structures on top of the mountain is hardly visible. Fish fossils have been found in large numbers on the mountaintops in this area, indicating support for the Great Flood that devastated the civilization between 10,000 and 14,000 years ago.*

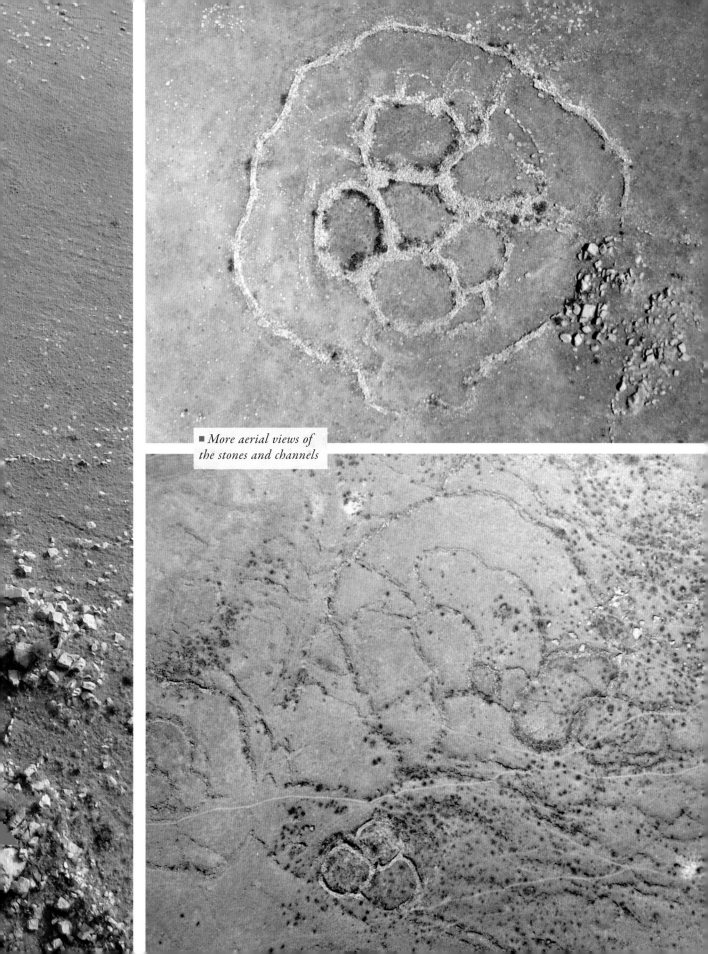

■ *More aerial views of the stones and channels*

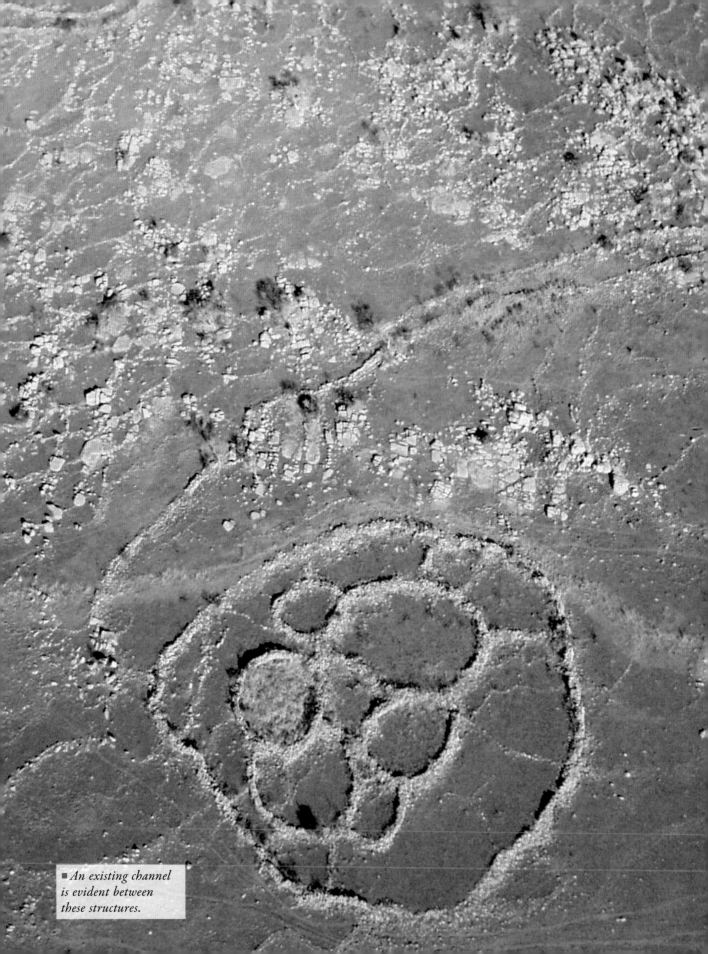

■ *An existing channel is evident between these structures.*

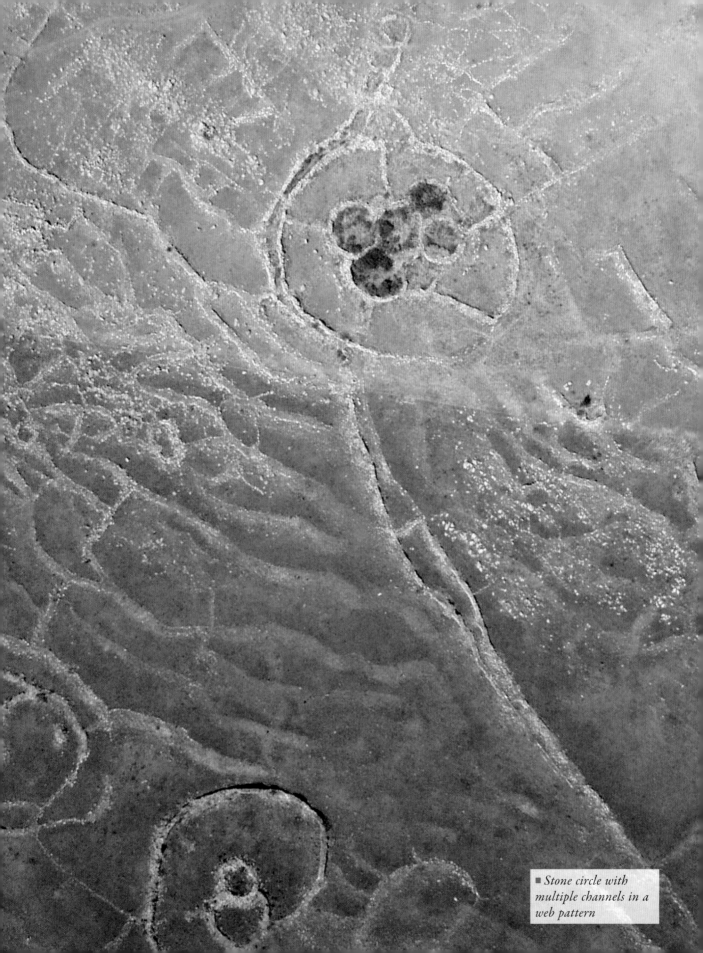

■ *A spectacular example of*
terraces, channels, and stone
circles covering several mountains
near Waterval Boven.

Monoliths

■ *Bird-shaped monolith, precursor to the Zimbabwe birds*

THE LOST CIVILIZATION was obsessed with monoliths. On the previous page is a breathtaking example of a bird-shaped monolith near Belfast, South Africa. There are obvious links to the well-known and mysterious Zimbabwe birds. Notice the wing that was once carved onto the lower body of the bird, greatly resembling the wings on the Zimbabwe birds, which are also placed low on the body. The images in this chapter offer a tiny glimpse at what lies scattered across most of southern Africa—an unimaginable number of tools and artifacts with many monoliths that will never be seen by most because of their remote locations. The image on page 206 shows the patina on a monolith which helps unlock the mystery of its age.

■ A strange accumulation of rectangular rocks carved and placed in some kind of arrangement. Meaning not established.

■ *Nick van Noordwyk, a property developer near Waterval Boven, who is 6 feet 6 inches tall, stands at the mysterious bird monolith indicating its size.*

■ *All pictures: The recurring shapes of carved stones at many of the ruins. Note the broader base with a long, narrow neck and head. I believe that these are the early and basic prototypes of what became the more refined Zimbabwe birds.*

■ *This is one of the greatest discoveries yet, which allows the author to speculate about the very old age of the ruins. The patina on this broken monolith has regrown to about a 2-millimeter thickness. He estimates that this kind of patina growth will not happen in less than 100,000 years. Although no scientific study exists to verify this, it is thought that this patina grows very slowly and shows only a microscopic layer every 1,000 years. The attempts to do patina growth studies with the Nelson Mandela Metropolitan University in Port Elizabeth have fallen through. More funding for high-level experiments is desperately needed to deliver unquestionable scientific evidence of the extreme age of these tools.*

■ *Slightly rounded monolith*

■ *Slightly rounded monolith*

■ *Polished monoliths and stones such as this one are linked directly to the Hindu worship of Lord Shiva. The author believes it has its origins in southern Africa and could be linked to the polishing of gold for the gods by the FIRST people of the vanished civilization.*

*A giant fallen monolith—
more than 3.5 meters tall*

■ *A 5-meter-tall monolith near Dullstroom, South Africa. Once again it resembles the basic shape of the prototype bird statues and monoliths, with a broad base that narrows to the top.*

■ *Johan Heine admires one of many built-in stones in the walls of certain ruins.*

■ *The author shows off two more examples of prototype Zimbabwe birds. One was accompanied by a strange anomalous stone tool for an as of yet unexplained purpose.*

■ *Another example of a built-in triangular stone in the wall of a large ruin. Triangular stones like this are associated with Hindu tradition and worship, but it seems that the Hindus also inherited their symbols from the FIRST people, the vanished civilization of southern Africa. I can say this with some certainty because of the ages of the ruins and the tools found in these ruins. It is, however, possible that the Hindu gold miners adapted some of the ruins to their own needs. This is evident from new entrances created in many of the original structures.*

■ *Another wonderful example of a bird statue*

■ *Some geologists are so baffled by the strange shapes of many of these tools and monoliths that they believe the ancient civilization must have had some kind of ability to mold them like clay by affecting their structural frequency, without actually carving them. If they understood the flow of energy as indicated by the stone circles, this notion is not as far-fetched as some may think.*

Giants, Tools, and Other Anomalies

■ *The author with the giant footprint. This mysterious footprint in a rock formation in South Africa stands about 120 centimeters (or 4 feet) tall and remains one of the best-kept secrets in South African archaeology.*

THE JOURNEY THROUGH the stone ruins has been filled with ancient unexplained phenomena, much of it shattering to the mainstream version of history. The best example of this is the giant footprint in rough granite, near Mpuluzi, South Africa, which is clearly evident in the opposite image. This is not a hoax. Most archaeologists and scholars simply shy away from this discovery, which is not the kind of response one would expect from a true scientist. We have to examine this phenomenon to help us understand the real history of this planet. When the Bible talks about the Anakim, or giants on Earth, maybe this is what it was referring to.

All of human history is filled with tales of giants. Many of our religious and sacred texts make repeated references to such humanoids of large proportion who once lived among ordinary humans. Whether it is the Bible and the reference to the giants in the land of Anak who made the people look like locusts at their feet, or the Native American references to the giants of Ohio and the mysterious Mounds of Ohio, it is almost impossible to find ancient cultures that do not talk about giants in their own past.

The mysterious Boskop skull that was found in South Africa in the very early 1900s clearly shows that there was a human species about 25% larger than we are today and would have stood about eight feet tall. The bone fragments were conveniently hidden in the vaults of various museums of South Africa for around 100 years. Such evidence would simply get in the way of a clean fairy-tale history of humanity that started with the beautiful Adam and Eve in the garden of Eden and led us to this point in time—right? The department of anthropology at the University of The Witwatersrand (WITS, as it is normally called) holds a specimen that comprises the top part of a femur with the hip joints well preserved. This fossil shows us that the being would have been as much as 50% larger than humans today.

One of the best examples of giants from a sacred text comes from the Mahabharata (1:8), which clearly outlines their existence in Hindu history.

Bhima was captivated by her and the seven months they enjoyed together seemed to pass as quickly . . . At the end of the seven months she gave birth to a son named Ghatotkaca. Within days of his birth the boy grew to youth-hood and he took on the terrible form of a Raksasa [giant]. His huge body was fearsome, with knotted muscles, a head as bald as a pot, terrible red eyes, a long pointed nose and ears like sharp arrows. His chest was broad and he stood as tall as a palm tree. (available at http://vedabase.com/en/mbk/1/8; accessed October 25, 2012)

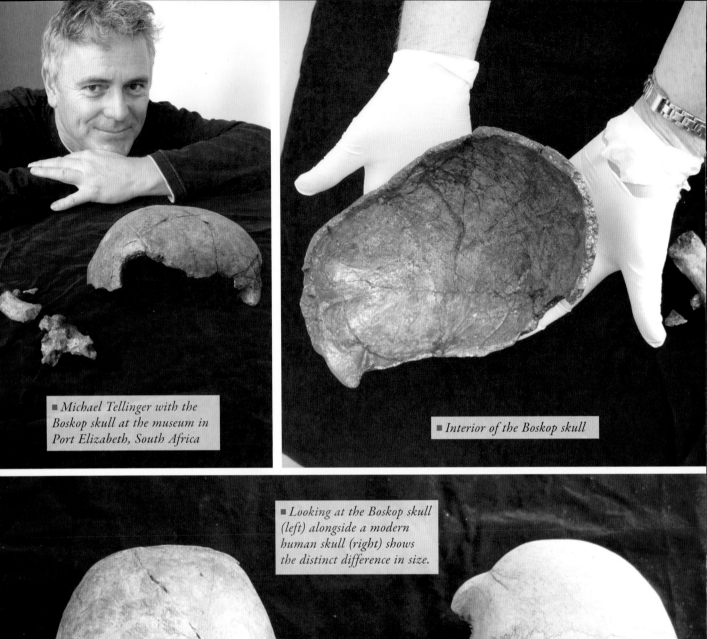

■ *Michael Tellinger with the Boskop skull at the museum in Port Elizabeth, South Africa*

■ *Interior of the Boskop skull*

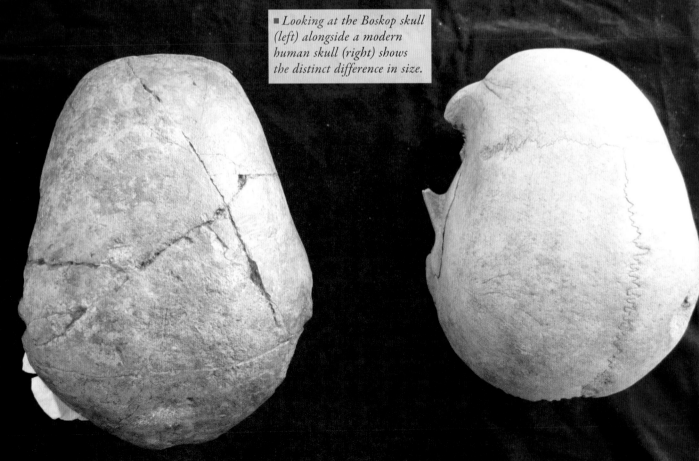

■ *Looking at the Boskop skull (left) alongside a modern human skull (right) shows the distinct difference in size.*

Klaus Dona, one of the world's leading researchers into unexplained mysteries of the past, made a sensational discovery of giant humanoid bones in Ecuador. He clearly shows that there were humanoids about 7.5 meters tall who walked the Earth. According to Dona the photographic and other evidence of this has been kept out of sight by the government and will continue to be until they feel fit to release it. Dona firmly believes that the giants he discovered would have left a footprint about the size of the spectacular example discovered in South Africa.

The giant footprint, an image of which opened this chapter, is undoubtedly my personal favorite example of giants in history. In *Geology of South Africa* this outcrop is called Mpuluzi batholith (granite) and the official dating of this rock produced dates of around 3.1 billion years. This is a real mystery that needs close scientific examination instead of ridicule by ignorant and fearful scholars. To date, only a small group of scholars have actually seen this site and marveled at this giant footprint. Some continue to claim—without ever having actually seen it—that it is a hoax or that it is simply a natural erosion pattern and insist that it is impossible to leave a footprint in granite because of the way granite is formed. The possibility that this is a natural erosion pattern is so unlikely and improbable that it does not even warrant an argument. Just speak to a scientist about the probability factor. Professor Pieter Wagener from the University of Port Elizabeth suggests that "there is a higher probability of little green men arriving from space and licking it out with their tongues, than being created by natural erosion."

Maybe we should start to question what we really know about geology; most of our scientific "truths" are mere assumptions without any real understanding of other forces of nature that we have not yet come to evaluate. These may include terra-forming, ancient epochs of sedimentation of a variety of material, and what happens to crushed granite slurry when left alone for a long period. While we keep learning new things about quantum physics, zero-point energy, the vacuum, and the laws of nature we will no doubt find new discoveries in our approach to geology. As we begin to understand more about the occult secrets of alchemy and transmutation of elements we will find those who have already mastered this knowledge—but unfortunately they are not part of the mainstream academic circles.

The footprint is located near the town of Mpaluzi in South Africa, close to the Swaziland border. It was discovered in 1912 by a farmer named Stoffel Coetzee while hunting. At the time this was a deeply remote part of South Africa known as the Eastern Transvaal, teeming with wildlife, including antelope and lions. The print remains in the same condition as it was when first discovered, and the possibility that this was a carved hoax is extremely low because of its remote location. Even today it is difficult to find. Yet it is imprinted in granite in a well-recognized geological part of South Africa and recorded on all geological maps—that is why this footprint is such an incredible mystery. It can be described as a phenocrystic granite, or coarse porphyritic granite, which underwent several different stages of cooling (therein lies the clue, I believe). As a result it is an interesting mixture of large and small granules. This is why granite companies are keen to mine this area—this granite will look really "pretty" when polished on some kitchen table top on the other side of the world.

I understand the argument very well—that it is impossible to create footprints in granite—and I do agree with all of that. So the question remains: How did this footprint get there? Because it is not a figment of our imagination—it is real and physical and we are not going to wish it away.

Another anomalous discovery is what Credo Mutwa calls Sacred Stones, but which have been called many things. An example can be seen in the image below. Most commonly called digging stones, they were supposedly used as weights attached to sticks for the purpose of digging for roots and food by Bantu settlers or hunter-gatherers. This is an ignorant and preposterous suggestion. The fact that hundreds of thousands of these stones lie scattered throughout southern Africa is a huge mystery, until we consider the use of vibrational frequency as energy. The holes in the stones are of different sizes and shapes and would generate a specific frequency when sound passes through them. They could well have been tools of the FIRST people in the construction of stone dwellings and mining of metals. Each stone has a specific function and was probably calibrated

■ *Sacred stone*

to the individual frequency of its operator. John Keely showed the same in 1888 when he pointed out that only he could use the vibration antigravity device, because it was calibrated to him. The device was a trumpetlike instrument—which is basically a tube with a hole in it—just like our Sacred Stones.

These stones, in all their forms, bring to the forefront the mysteries of our human past. Open your eyes, be a true scientist, do not fear what you might find, and do not be afraid to share your knowledge with others—although they may ridicule you simply because they do not understand and have little knowledge of the subject.

■ *A small statuette carved out of stone, about 15 centimeters tall, found among stone tools at Waterval Boven. According to our estimate, this is by far the oldest statue on Earth.*

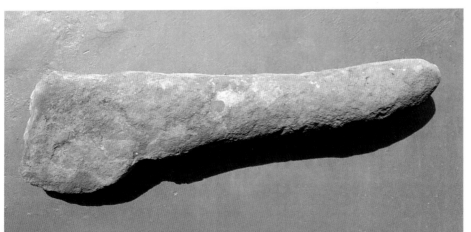

■ *Large ritual stone phallus, 45 centimeters long, found next to a stone circle ruin on top of a mountain among many other Stone Age tools.*

■ *The beauty of our Earth conceals mysteries beyond our understanding.*

Conclusion

THIS BOOK WAS written and compiled purely to present a few highlights and the mystery of our ancient history. The collection of spectacular photographs leaves no doubt that something strange was happening in southern Africa many thousands of years ago. Our current civilization is only beginning to see the tip of the proverbial iceberg of our ancient past. I trust that this will stimulate you to ask more questions, explore more, and embark on a journey of discovery more fascinating than you could have ever imagined.

If you feel that this has whetted your appetite, or left you with hunches you would like to see verified, consider reading my book *Slave Species of the Gods.* In it I discuss what the Sumerian tablets say about the creation of human-kind, gods on Earth, the interconnection of all cultures, and how the universal human quest for gold—and the need to enslave others—came to pass. It might sound like science fiction, but, as the stunning visual images presented in this book attest, the truth is here before our very eyes.

Resources

A LARGE DISPLAY of unique artifacts and photographs can be viewed at the Stone Circle Bistro & Museum in Waterval Boven, Mpumalanga, South Africa.

The author has initiated a variety of tours to the ruins and Adam's Calendar. To find out more about the tours, e-mail:

contact@zuluplanet.com

To stay up to date with the author's work and research, join his mailing list on his website:

www.michaeltellinger.com

Bibliography

Ancient Artifact Preservation Society. "Brazilian Stonehenge Found." www.aaapf .org/scripts/prodView.asp?idproduct=54 (undated article; accessed October 22, 2012).

Anitei, Stefan. "World's Oldest Ritual Site Found in Africa." Softpedia. http://news. softpedia.com/news/Oldest-Ritual-Site-Found-in-Africa-41459.shtml (undated article; accessed October 22, 2012).

Ascension Alchemy. "David Hudson's Collected Lectures." www.asc-alchemy.com/ hudson.html (undated page; accessed October 22, 2012).

Bent, J. Theodore. *The Ruined Cities of Mashonaland*. New edition. Rhodesia: Books of Rhodesia, 1969.

Bong, Wun Chok. *The Gods' Machines: From Stonehenge to Crop Circles*. N.p.: Frog Books, 2008.

Braden, Gregg. *The Divine Matrix: Bridging Time, Space, Miracles, and Belief*. Carlsbad, Calif.: Hay House, 2008.

Bramley, William. *The Gods of Eden*. New York: Avon Books, 1993.

Brown, Dan. *The Da Vinci Code*. New York: Anchor, 2009.

Brown, Kyle S., Curtis W. Marean, Andy I. R. Herries, et al. "Fire as an Engineering Tool of Early Modern Humans." *Science* 325, no. 5942 (August 14, 2009): 859–62.

Cruttenden, Walter. *Lost Star of Myth and Time*. Pittsburgh: St. Lynn's Press, 2005.

Dona, Klaus. *The Klaus Dona Chronicles: Secret World 1*. DVD. www.unsolved-mysteries .info (accessed October 24, 2012).

Fagan, Brian. *Time Detectives: How Archaeologists Use Technology to Recapture the Past*. New York: Simon & Schuster, 1996.

Fage, J. D., and Roland Oliver, eds. *Papers in African Prehistory*. Cambridge, England: Cambridge University Press, 1970.

Flam, Faye. "Sumerian Dictionary to Decipher Ancient Texts." *Philadelphia Inquirer,*

July 24, 2002. http://news.nationalgeographic.com/news/2002/07/0723_020724_cuneiform.html (accessed October 23, 2012).

Gardner, Laurence. *Lost Secrets of the Sacred Ark*. New Edition. Salisbury, England: Element Books, 2004.

Heine, Johan, and Michael Tellinger. *Adam's Calendar: Discovering the Oldest Man-made Structure on Earth*. Seattle, Wash.: Compendium, Inc., 2008.

Hromnik, Cyril A. "Ancient Indian Religious Astronomy in the Stone Ruins of Komatiland, South Africa." *Astronomical Society of Southern Africa, Monthly Notes* 55 (1996): 69–77.

———. *Indo-Africa: Towards a New Understanding of the History of Sub-Saharan Africa*. Cape Town, South Africa: Juta & Co. Ltd., 1981.

Joburg: Official Website of the City of Johannesburg. "[Revil] Mason Replaces Boer History" www.joburg.org.za/index.php?option=com_content&task=view&id=4685&Itemid=266 (article dated December 22, 2009; accessed October 22, 2012).

Kritzinger, Ann. "The Makorakoza of Zimbabwe: Centuries of Prospecting in Gold-Hosting Dolerites." *Prospecting and Mining Journal* 77, no. 9 (May 2008).

LaViolette, Paul. *Genesis of the Cosmos: The Ancient Science of Continuous Creation*. Rochester, Vt.: Bear & Company, 2004.

Nature. "The Indo-Sumerian Seals Deciphered: Discovering Sumerians of Indus Valley as Phoenicians, Barats, Goths and Famous Vedic Aryans, 3100–2300 BC." 116 (September 5, 1925): 351–52.

Sitchin, Zecharia. *The Lost Book of Enki*. Rochester, Vt.: Bear & Company, 2001.

Sullivan, Brenda. *Spirit of the Rocks*. Pretoria, South Africa: Human & Rousseau, 1995.

Summers, Roger. *Ancient Ruins and Vanished Civilizations of Southern Africa*. N.p.: Bulpin, 1971.

———. "The Rhodesian Iron Age." In Fage and Oliver, eds. *Papers in African Prehistory*. Cambridge, England: Cambridge University Press, 1970.

Tucker, Linda. *Children of the Sun God: Journey with the White Lions into the Heart of Human Evolution*. Johannesburg, South Africa: Mail & Guardian, 2001.

BOOKS OF RELATED INTEREST

Slave Species of the Gods
The Secret History of the Anunnaki
and Their Mission on Earth
by Michael Tellinger

The Anunnaki Chronicles
A Zecharia Sitchin Reader
by Zecharia Sitchin
Edited by Janet Sitchin

The 12th Planet
by Zecharia Sitchin

There Were Giants Upon the Earth
Gods, Demigods, and Human Ancestry:
The Evidence of Alien DNA
by Zecharia Sitchin

The Lost Book of Enki
Memoirs and Prophecies of an Extraterrestrial God
by Zecharia Sitchin

DNA of the Gods
The Anunnaki Creation of Eve and the Alien Battle for Humanity
by Chris H. Hardy, Ph.D.

Black Genesis
The Prehistoric Origins of Ancient Egypt
by Robert Bauval and Thomas Brophy, Ph.D.

Forbidden History
Prehistoric Technologies, Extraterrestrial Intervention,
and the Suppressed Origins of Civilization
Edited by J. Douglas Kenyon

Inner Traditions • Bear & Company
P.O. Box 388
Rochester, VT 05767
1-800-246-8648
www.InnerTraditions.com

Or contact your local bookseller